APPLYING SKILLS

for Foundation GCSE Maths Exams

Michael White

Elmwood Press

ii

First published 2012 by
Elmwood Press
80 Attimore Road
Welwyn Garden City
Herts. AL8 6LP
Tel. 01707 333232

ISBN 9781 906 622 220

Numerical answers are published in a separate book

Typeset and illustrated by Domex e-Data Pvt. Ltd.
Printed in Slovenia by Ednas Print

PREFACE

This stand-alone book provides banks of questions which have been written to complement any GCSE resources.

The questions focus on assessment objectives AO2 and AO3, ie. selecting appropriate methods, solving functional problems and explaining methods fully.

A '*' has been placed by each question number as found in GCSE examination papers because every type of question in this book encourages quality of written communication (QWC).

There are 28 sets of questions which can be used throughout the GCSE course or as more of a revisional aid. They may be tackled initially by groups of students to explore and discuss strategies or worked at individually. The majority of the sets of questions involve a mixture of topics which is essential if the students are to recall and select appropriate techniques. Some exercises are specific to Number, Algebra, Geometry or Statistics only.

Users of the main Elmwood Press Foundation GCSE Maths textbook will find links to this book in the answer book for 'Applying Skills for Foundation GCSE Maths Exams'.

Michael White

CONTENTS LIST

PART ONE

* 1 Kate saves £7 each week for 18 weeks. Her grandparents give her £50 for her birthday. Kate wants to buy a camera which costs £225.

    (a) Can Kate afford to buy the camera?

    (b) If yes, how much money does she have left over?

        If no, how much more money does she need to save?

* 2 Two clubs put on firework displays.

    The Greenbank club sell 900 tickets at £6 each.

    They spend £2600 on the fireworks. Morley rugby club sell 1250 tickets at £8 each. The cost of their fireworks is £5900.

    Which club makes the most profit and by how much?

* 3 Darren is planning a day trip to the beach for his football club.

    The costs are given below:

Coach (55 seats)	£450 per coach
Food	£14 per person
Extra costs	£35

    A ticket for the day trip costs £24. Ninety-five people buy a ticket.
    Does Darren get enough money to pay for the coach travel, food and extra costs?

* 4

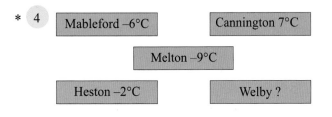

Mableford –6°C		Cannington 7°C
Melton –9°C		
Heston –2°C		Welby ?

The difference between the temperatures at Melton and Cannington is the same as the difference between the temperatures at Heston and Welby.

Write down the **two** possible temperatures at Welby.

* 5 After a large party, Fran has 99 empty wine bottles and 106 empty beer bottles. She puts all the bottles into boxes.

> A wine box can hold 6 bottles

> A beer box can hold 12 bottles

Her friend Morgan has a van which has room for 25 boxes.
Will all the boxes fit into the van?

* 6

Ben and Louise each have a market stall. Ben buys 150 sunglasses for £900 and sells them all at £8 each. Louise buys 120 sunglasses for £600 and sells 110 of them at £9 each. Who makes the larger profit and by how much?

* 7 A factory worker works on an assembly line making magnifying glasses.

She gets £40 each day plus £5 for every 200 magnifying glasses she deals with. One week she works for five days and deals with 1200 magnifying glasses.
How much does she earn?

* 8 Matt goes into college on 4 days of each week. His mother gives him £20 each week to buy his lunches. His lunch costs him £4 each day.

He saves the money left over each week throughout the year (term time only: 38 weeks).
How much money does he save in total?

* 9   The boss of a small firm wants to give each person in the firm a hand painted Easter egg.

> **Plan A**
> £9 for every
> 5 eggs

> **Plan B**
> £2 for each egg. 1 free egg
> for every 20 eggs bought.

The boss needs to buy an egg for each of 90 people.

Which is cheaper – plan A or plan B? Give reasons for your answer.

* 10   A group of 10 people do the National Lottery. Six more people join the group. After a few weeks, the group win £33600. The money is shared out equally between the people in the group.

One of these people decides to share out his winnings equally between his wife, himself and his three children.

His youngest child spends £93 on computer games. How much money does this child have left over from the winnings?

* 11

Jack's freezer is usually at a temperature of –25°C. Jack goes to bed at 10 p.m. and comes down to the kitchen in the morning at 7 a.m. The freezer breaks down at 11 p.m. The temperature rises 4°C each hour. The food in the freezer will be ruined if the temperature goes above 0°C for more than two hours.

Jack checks the freezer as soon as he comes down to the kitchen in the morning. Is the food in the freezer still OK or is it ruined?

Give reasons for your answer.

* 12 A basketball arena has room for 20000 people plus
     overflow space for an extra $\frac{1}{10}$ of this number of people.

     There are 12 gates to this arena.
     For one match, the table below shows how
     many people went through each gate.

Gate 1 1273	Gate 2 1614	Gate 3 1389	Gate 4 1418
Gate 5 2172	Gate 6 1905	Gate 7 2712	Gate 8 1849
Gate 9 2178	Gate 10 1819	Gate 11 1567	Gate 12 1872

Was there enough room in the arena for this
number of people?

Explain your answer.

Ⓜ MIXED 1

* 1

Electricity Bill	
New reading	65248 units
Old reading	64897 units
Price per unit	36p

This is part of Ryan's electricity bill. Work out how much Ryan has to pay for his electricity.

* 2 Mia wants to plant 144 trees in rows. She wants the number of trees in each row to equal the number of rows.

(a) Explain or draw how she would place the trees.

(b) Mia changes her mind. She now decides the number of rows should be four times greater than the number of trees in each row. Explain or draw how she would now place the trees.

* 3 Carson's mother wants him back home by 7:45 p.m. for a meal. Carson is at a friend's house. Carson wants to play squash before going home and needs to visit a local store to buy some chocolates. Look at the table below and work out the latest time he can leave his friend's house so that he gets back home in time for the meal.

Walk from friend's house to squash court	25 minutes
Change for squash	5 minutes
Play squash	45 minutes
Clean and change into normal clothes	10 minutes
Walk from squash court to store	15 minutes
Buy chocolates	10 minutes
Walk from store to home	20 minutes

6

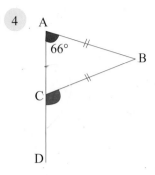

Find the value of angle BCD.
You must give all your reasons.

Find the value of angle QRS.
You must give all your reasons.

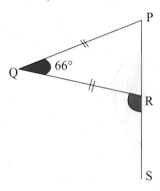

5   Owen and Stella have always wanted to visit
the Grand Canyon in the USA. They decide
to save together for a holiday for two in
the USA which will cost a total of £6100.

Owen's take-home pay each month is £1463.
He shares a flat. The table below shows what
he has to pay out each month. He saves
the rest of his money.

Rent	£328
Electricity	£22
Gas	£18
Water	£13
Phone	£40
Council tax	£25
Food/entertainment	£400

Stella lives at home with her parents. Her take-home pay each month is £1220.
Each month she gives her parents £400, pays £35 for her phone and spends £160
on entertainment. She saves the rest of her money.

How many months will it take Owen and Stella to save enough money for
the USA holiday?

* 6 Katya hires a car. The cost is worked out by the formula below:

cost = fixed charge + cost per mile × number of miles

The fixed charge is £65. The cost per mile is 20p.
How many miles did Katya travel if
the cost of hiring the car was £125?

* 7 Mrs Thomas needs help at home. A nurse visits every 6 days and
a social worker visits every 8 days. The nurse and social worker
both visit on July 19th. On what date will both the nurse and
social worker next visit Mrs Thomas on the same day?

* 8 Alexa and 3 friends need to book their summer holiday.
They plan to share two twin rooms at the Regala hotel.
The cost of the rooms is shown below.

	6th June– 3rd July		4th July– 7th August		8th August– 12th September		13th September– 15th October	
	7 nights	14 nights	7 nights	14 nights	7 nights	14 nights	7 nights	14 nights
Single room	£525	£675	£595	£765	£625	£780	£575	£720
Double room	£605	£775	£675	£865	£705	£880	£645	£800
Twin Room	£605	£785	£685	£880	£715	£895	£645	£810

Each price shown above is the price per person.
Alexa and her friends wish to go on 15th August
for 14 nights.

Alexa pays a deposit of £245.
She has 5 months to save the rest of the money.
How much money does she need to save each
month to be able to pay for this holiday?

* 9

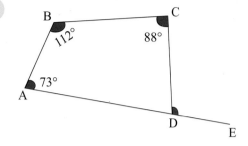

Find the value of angle CDE.
You mush give all your reasons.

* 10 Logan, Anjali, Naomi and Gavin want to see a film
at the cinema. A ticket at the Cresswall Cinema is £7.60.
A ticket at the Albert Cinema is £6.50.

The friends can get to the Cresswall Cinema by bus for £7.90
return. There is no bus to the Albert Cinema.

They can get a taxi to either cinema.

> Cost of taxi   £1.30 per mile.

Which cinema and type of transport will be the cheapest option
for the 4 friends if the Cresswall Cinema is 12 miles away and
the Albert Cinema is 14 miles away? Explain your reasons.

Ⓝ NUMBER 2

* ① Evan is replacing some fencing. He buys the following items.
The cost of each item is also given.

4 fence panels	£12.99 each
5 posts	£7.50 each
2 packets of screws	£3.85 each

Evan pays with five £20 notes. How much change will he get?

* ②

Brianna makes cakes for a tea shop. She uses $\frac{2}{5}$ kg of sugar for each cake.
Brianna buys the sugar in 5 kg bags.

How much cakes can Brianna make with the sugar from one 5 kg bag?

* ③ Anya earns £560 each week. She works very hard so on 8th March she is given a 4% pay rise.

On the 7th May she is paid a bonus of £850.

How much does Anya earn in total between 8th March and 23rd May?

* 4   Marcus wants to buy an i-pod. He tries three different stores.

Techshow	Marleys	E-market
£260 $\frac{1}{5}$ off	£210	£250 15% reduction

Which store offers the lowest price for Marcus?
Show your working out.

* 5   Asha spends $\frac{1}{5}$ of her money on a mask and $\frac{1}{4}$ of her money on food.

What fraction of her money has she now got left?

* 6   A factory is protected by two guards. Guard 1 leaves the main office and returns to the office every 15 minutes.

Guard 2 leaves the main office and returns to the office every 18 minutes.

If both guards leave the main office at 10 p.m., when will they next be back at the office at the same time?

* 7   Copy and complete the bill shown below:

AUTO TYRES			
Item	Number	Price per item	Cost
Tyre	4	£41.20	
Air filter	1	£15.80	
Brake pad	2	£16.50	
Labour: 2 hours at £41.20 per hour			
VAT (Value Added Tax) at 20%			
		Total cost	

* 8   Jocelyn receives some money from her uncle.
She spends $\frac{1}{5}$ of the money on clothes.
She spends 40% of the money on a computer.
She spends $\frac{3}{8}$ of the money on a holiday.
If she spent £192 on the clothes, how much
money did she have left after all the spending?

* 9   Austin wants to invest £2000 in a bank for 2 years.
He looks at the two deals below:

ZPN Bank
5% per annum compound interest

Reece Bank
6% per annum simple interest
The bank charges a fee of 10% of the interest made when all the money is withdrawn

Austin will take out all the money
after 2 years.

Which deal is the best
for Austin and by how much?

* 10 In September 2011 Brooklyn takes out a mortgage of £70000 at a fixed rate of 4.14% per annum. The fixed rate deal lasts for 5 years.

If she pays the money back early, she has to pay a penalty as shown below:

Pay back within:	Penalty (% of original mortgage)
1 year	5%
2 years	4%
3 years	3%
4 years	2%
5 years	1%

Brooklyn pays back all the money in March 2015.
How much money is the penalty she has to pay?

* 11 During his career, Ryan wins 48 formula One races. $\frac{2}{3}$ of these races are in Europe. Out of these, $\frac{5}{8}$ were during the last 5 years of his career.

How many Formula One races in Europe did Ryan win during the last 5 years of his career?

* 12

1 litre
£2.20

2 litres
£3.70

1.5 litres
£2.90

The prices of freshly squeezed orange juice are shown above.
Lian needs to buy 5 litres of this orange juice.
Which cartons should she buy so that she spends the least amount of money?

Ⓜ MIXED 2

* 1   In Clegg's factory, a machine takes $8\frac{1}{2}$ minutes to fill a box with chocolates and to wrap the box. The machine starts up at 06:00. Will the machine deal with 30 boxes by 10:00? Give reasons for your answer.

* 2   This shows the amount of fuel in Avery's car.

Each bar shows $\frac{1}{8}$ of the petrol in the car's tank.

A full petrol tank contains 40 litres.

A litre of petrol costs £1.68.

How much money will it cost Avery to fill the petrol tank up completely?

* 3   Brandon lays 150 bricks in one hour. On Tuesday he has a 20 minute morning break and a 45 minute lunch break. He starts work at 8 a.m. and has to lay 900 bricks.

At what time should Brandon finish laying all these bricks?

* 4   Mason, Alyssa and Rahul are training on the running track at their local athletics club.

The table shows how long they each take to complete one lap of the track.

Mason	9 minutes
Alyssa	8 minutes
Rahul	6 minutes

They leave the start line at the same time and run for 90 minutes in total.
When they are next all at the start line at **the same time**, how much longer do they run for before completing the 90 minutes?

14

* 5 A cookbook gives the rule below for roasting a joint of beef.

$$T = 25W + 30$$

Where T is the cooking time in minutes and W is the weight of the beef.

(a) Dylan has a 2.5 kg joint of beef. If he starts cooking it at 11:30 a.m., will it be ready to eat by 12:45 p.m? Explain your reasons.

(b) Ava has a joint of beef which takes 1 hour 45 minutes to cook. Work out the weight of this joint of beef.

* 6 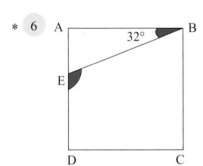 ABCD is a square.

Work out the size of angle BED.

Give reasons for your answer.

* 7 If a person does not pay the year's tax bill by 31st January, a penalty payment at £100 must be made.

For every month after 31st January that the tax bill is not paid, the person will have to pay an extra 2% of the tax bill.

Deven has a tax bill of £3800. How much must he pay in total if he pays the bill on 10th March?

* 8 There are 240 students in the Sixth Form at Horton Hill High School. 60% of these students go to the nearby Glastonbury festival. $\frac{2}{3}$ of these people who go to the festival share a tent. $\frac{1}{2}$ of these tent people are male.

What fraction of all the Sixth Form students are females who share a tent at the festival?

* 9   Ella wants to buy 3 kg of cherries.
The local shop sells cherries in 3 different sizes.

£2.20
1 kg

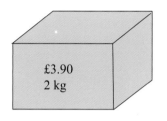

£3.90
2 kg

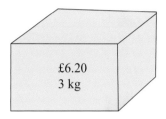

£6.20
3 kg

What is the cheapest way of Ella buying 3 kg of cherries?
Show all your working out.

* 10   Cole owns an i-phone.
He pays a monthly contract of £35 as
set out below:

£35 plan
includes: 500 minutes phone calls Unlimited texts
Each extra minute phone call: 21.5 p

In April, Cole makes 628 minutes of phone calls and 802 texts.
How much does Cole have to pay for his i-phone at the end of April?

* 1

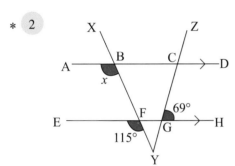

Work out the size of the angle marked *x*.
You must give reasons for each step in your working.

* 2

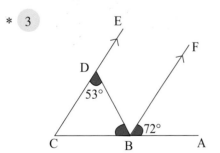

Work out the size of the angle marked *x*.
Give reasons for your answer.

* 3

Calculate the size of angle CBD.

You must give reasons for each step in your working.

* 4   Work out the size of the angle marked *x*.
       Give reasons for your answer.

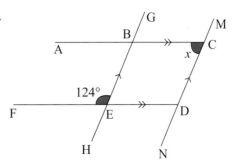

* 5   Calculate the size of angle ABE.
       You must give reasons to explain your answer.

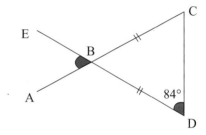

* 6

Copy and shade two more squares so that this pattern has rotational symmetry of order 4.

18

* 7 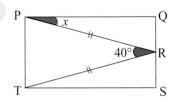 PQST is a rectangle.

PRT is an isosceles triangle.
Work out the size of the angle marked x.
Give reasons for your answer.

* 8 A shape in a computer game needs to be moved on the screen.

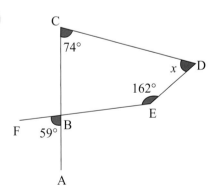

The following instructions are used:

(a) Rotate the shape 90° anticlockwise about A.

(b) Translate the shape with $\begin{pmatrix} -5 \\ -1 \end{pmatrix}$

(c) Now translate the shape with $\begin{pmatrix} 0 \\ -4 \end{pmatrix}$

Draw the shape on squared paper.
Show the new position of the shape.

* 9 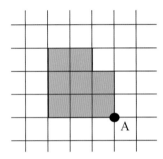 Calculate the size of the angle marked x.
You must give reasons to explain your answer.

* 10

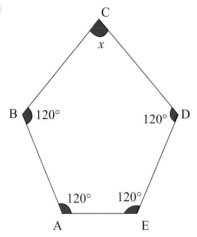

ABCDE is a pentagon.

Calculate the size of the angle marked x.

Give reasons for your answer.

* 11

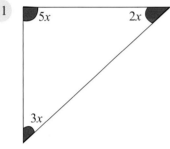

Work out the size of the smallest angle in this triangle.

* 12 Draw a design which uses the shape P shown opposite and two further shapes. One of these shapes must be an enlargement of shape P with scale factor 2. The other shape must be an enlargement of shape P with scale factor 3.

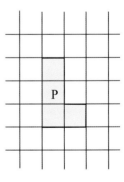

Ⓜ MIXED 3

* 1 Aaron needs to buy a new washing machine.
He finds the machine he wants in three different stores.
The prices are shown below:

DAWSONS	WASHWELL	LECTROSTORE
£420	£499.99	£500
+VAT	(including VAT)	15% discount then +VAT

Which store offers the cheapest deal for Aaron if VAT = 20%?
You must show all your working out.

* 2 A 500 ml drink called 'orange explosion' contains 300 ml of water.
Would 750 ml of the same drink contain more or less than 450 ml of water?
Explain your answer.

* 3 Chester and his family are going to the theatre to watch a show.

The ticket prices are shown below:

Adult	£24.50
(Senior citizen discount	10%)
(Student discount	10%)
Child (16 and under)	£15

There are two adults, one student and two children aged 14 and 11.
Chester pays for the tickets in advance with his credit card.
This means that he has to pay an extra 50p for each ticket.
How much does Chester pay in total for all the tickets?

* 4 Paige has a piece of ribbon. She uses $\frac{2}{5}$ of the ribbon on a present for her mother and another $\frac{1}{3}$ of the ribbon on a gift for her sister. She needs another 55 cm of ribbon for a final present.

  Does she have enough ribbon left for this final present if she started with 240 cm of ribbon?

* 5 24 tubes of red and blue paint are mixed in the ratio 3:5.

  18 tubes of blue and yellow paint are mixed in the ratio 2:7.

  How many tubes of blue paint were used in total?

* 6 Mr Kenwood is working out the cost of his next gas bill.

Gas Meter Readings
Previous reading: 31789
Present reading : 33004

  He has to pay:

  16.8p for the first 400 units used

  11.2p for the remaining units used

  How much will Mr Kenwood have to pay for this gas bill?

* 7 A person pays less car insurance
if no claims are made for money
from the insurance firm. This is
a percentage known as a
'no claims' discount.

Adam's full annual car insurance
is £1840. He has a 60%
no claims discount.

Unfortunately he has a car accident
and his no claims discount is
reduced to 20%. How much *more*
money will he now have to pay for his car insurance for that year?

* 8 Ten friends plan a day trip to
the seaside. They can get there
by minibus taxi or by train.
The prices are shown below:

Train	£15.60 day return

Minibus taxi for 10 people
£103.50

Each friend has a train railcard which gives each
one of them a 30% discount.

(a) The minibus appears to be cheaper.
How much will each friend save compared to using the train?

(b) On the day, one friend is ill. The other 9 friends still have to use
the taxi. This is now more expensive for each of them than using the train.
By how much?

* 9 Blake and Maya help Lauren to decorate a room for her grandmother.
They are paid a total of £712 for doing the job. Blake receives $\frac{1}{6}$ of the money.

The rest of the money is split in the ratio 4:7 between Maya and Lauren.
How much more money does Maya get than Blake?

* 10 Sophia likes to talk a lot! She decides
to do a sponsored 'silence' to raise money
for charity. Her sponsor form is shown
below. She manages to stay silent for
14 hours.

She wants to raise £100. Does
she succeed? Explain your reasons.

Name	Amount
Megan	50p per hour
Jane	25p per hour
Mum	£20
Aditi	£5
Kimberly	10p per hour
Dad	£20
Jason	50p per hour for the first 10 hours only
Mr Reed	£5
Auntie Molly	30p per hour for the first 12 hours then 60p per hour
Kevin	10p per hour
Sabina	£1
Shui	£1
Ian	£5 for the first 10 hours then an extra 20% if more than 10 hours
Mrs Cole	10p per hour
Aida	£1 for every complete 3 hours
Mrs Weaver	£2
Zoe	20p per hour
Amelia	25p per hour for the first 8 hours only
Ayden	£5
Mr Henry	40p per hour for the first 6 hours then 80p per hour

ⓢ | **STATISTICS 1**

* 1 Jaden found out which colour straws
had been used in a restaurant during
Thursday evening. The findings are
shown in the tally chart below.

Colour	Tally
Blue	ⅠⅠⅠⅠ ⅠⅠⅠⅠ 11
Yellow	ⅠⅠⅠⅠ 111
Red	ⅠⅠⅠⅠ ⅠⅠⅠⅠ 1111
White	1111
Purple	ⅠⅠⅠⅠ ⅠⅠⅠⅠ 1
Green	ⅠⅠⅠⅠ 11

(a) Draw a suitable chart or diagram to show Jaden's findings.

(b) How many straws were used in total during Thursday evening?

(c) Mackenzie went to the restaurant on Thursday evening
and had a glass of coke. What is the probability that she had
a purple straw?

* 2 Angelina wants to find out
what type of music the people
in her tutor group at school
like best.

Design a data collection
sheet that Angelina can use
to collect this information.

* 3 The weights of 16 footballers in a squad are given below (in kg).

72 66 71 84 75 81 69 68

91 70 72 66 82 77 64 73

(a) Copy and complete this grouped frequency table for these weights.

Weight (W)	Tally	Frequency
$60 \leq W < 70$		
$70 \leq W < 80$		
$80 \leq W < 90$		
$90 \leq W < 100$		

(b) Draw a suitable chart or graph to show these weights.

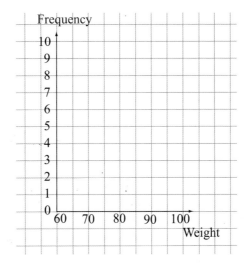

* 4 125 students in year 9 study French, German or Spanish.
22 girls study French. There are 70 girls in total.
25 boys do German. There are 42 students doing Spanish,
of which 12 are boys.

How many students in total study German? (Hint: draw a two-way table if you are confused then fill in the numbers you are given.

For example:

	French	German	Spanish	Total
Boys		25	12	
Girls	22		30	70
Total			42	125

Now work out the empty spaces to find the answer to the question.)

* 5   Write down a question which may have been used in a survey to give the frequency table shown below:

Animal	Number of people
Lion	58
Elephant	91
Leopard	32
Giraffe	68
Kangaroo	47

* 6   58 people on a coach stop at a pub for lunch. There are 32 women. 14 of these women have lasagne for lunch. 10 men have steak pie and 5 men have chicken curry. The total number of people having steak pie is 22. If each person has lasagne, steak pie or chicken curry, how many people have chicken curry in total?

* 7.   Hayden is in charge of bungee jumping for three months at a holiday resort in Australia.

In the stem and leaf diagram below, Hayden records, how many people bungee jump each week.

```
0 | 8
1 | 1 1 2 4 4 7 8        Key 1|4 means 14 people
2 | 1 3 3 3 6
```

Calculate

(a) the mean number of people who bungee jump each week.

(b) the median number of people.

(c) the modal number of people.

(d) the range for the number of people.

* 8 Bella runs a shop which sells pasties. She records how many steak pasties and vegetable pasties are sold on each of five days of the week.

This information is shown in the bar chart below.

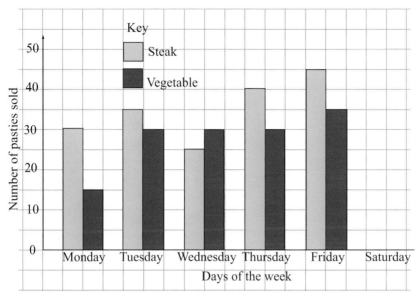

(a) How many vegetable pasties were sold on Friday?

(b) On which day of the week were more vegetable pasties sold than steak pasties?

(c) On Saturday Bella sold 50 steak pasties and 45 vegetable pasties.
Copy then complete the bar chart with this information.

(d) From Monday to Saturday, how many more steak pasties did Bella sell than vegetable pasties?

Show your working out.

* 9 Henry records the type of motorbike he sees at a motorbike show. He sees 90 in total.
The findings are shown in the table below.

Type	Frequency
Kawasaki	16
Yamaha	8
Harley Davidson	14
Ducati	12
Honda	?
Suzuki	20

Represent this information in a suitable diagram or chart.

∗ 10 The range of the numbers below is 16.

   25   29   32   33   ?

   Write down the two possible values for
   the unknown number.

∗ 11 100 students go on a school trip.
     As soon as they arrive, they each
     have a drink of either water, coke or
     juice. 24 of the 57 boys drink coke.
     27 girls drink water.

     A total of 24 students drink juice.
     One third of these are girls.

     Find the total number of students
     who had a drink of water.

∗ 12 The bar chart below shows the monthly rainfall in
     Porto for the summer months. This table shows
     the monthly rainfall in Barcelona for the same months.

Month	May	June	July	Aug	Sep	Oct
Rainlfall (mm)	40	35	15	20	35	55

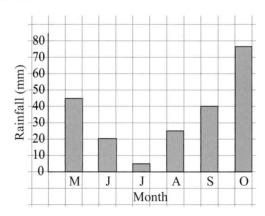

(a) Draw a suitable chart for Barcelona on a second set of axes.

(b) Compare the rainfall of the two cities.

MIXED 4

* 1   Kaitlyn needs to make the same cake in each of the four weeks in February.
The cake recipe for 12 people includes:

210 g	plain chocolate
270 g	icing sugar
240 g	butter
6	egg whites
465 ml	thick cream
180 g	flour

Each week she needs to make the cake for 8 people. She decides to buy
the icing sugar, flour and plain chocolate for all the cakes at the start of February.

Each of these ingredients is sold in two sizes in her local store
as shown below.

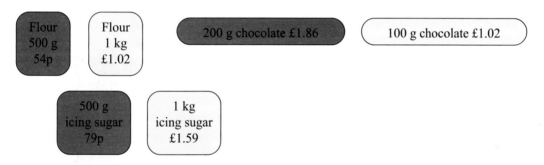

Flour
500 g
54p

Flour
1 kg
£1.02

200 g chocolate £1.86

100 g chocolate £1.02

500 g
icing sugar
79p

1 kg
icing sugar
£1.59

Calculate the least amount she must spend on the icing sugar,
flour and plain chocolate.

* 2   In 2011 the ratio of old factories to modern factories is
2:3 in parts of the UK. There are actually 17250 modern
factories.

In 2012, half the old factories are knocked down
and rebuilt as modern factories.

What is the new ratio of old factories to
modern factories?

* **3** Brody wants to find out how many magazines people read.
He needs to design a questionnaire. Make up
a suitable question for Brody's questionnaire.

* **4**

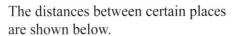

Lines PQ and RS are parallel.

Calculate the size of angle BDE.

Give reasons for your answer.

* **5** Morgan sells wine. She receives 20%
commission on any wine that
she sells. Last week she travels
from York to Sheffield then to
Nottingham then back to York.
She can claim 21.5p travel
expenses for every mile that
she covers.

The distances between certain places
are shown below.

York				
58	Sheffield			
87	35	Derby		
82	28	7	Nottingham	
25	40	74	67	Leeds

Morgan sells this amount of wine in each place.

Sheffield £320

Nottingham £794

York £283

How much money does Morgan get in total
from her wine commission and travel expenses?

* 6   One day Suraj sees 4 types of bird.

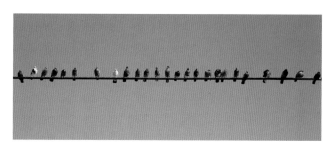

80% of the birds are starlings.
The remaining birds are pigeons,
bluetits and magpies in
the ratio 7:3:2.

If Suraj sees 15 bluetits,
how many starlings does he see?

* 7   In a TV game show, each player is given 25 points to start with.
Each player scores 4 more points when a question is answered
correctly. The total number of points T is given by the formula

$$T = 25 + 4n$$

Where n is the number of correct answers given.

If Tristan scores 61 points in total, how many correct answers did he give?

* 8   The chart below shows some train times.

Westbury	1542	1619	1719	1758	1837	1920
Trowbridge	1551	1628	1728	1807	1846	1929
Bath	1601	1638	1738	1817	1856	1939
Bristol	1620	1658	1758	1836	1915	1958

Bristol	2018	2047	2118	2207	2218	2305
Bath	2036	2105	2136	2225	2236	2323
Trowbridge	2046	2115	2146	2235	2246	2333
Westbury	2057	2126	2157	2246	2257	2344

Natalia lives in Westbury. It takes her 20 minutes
to walk from her home to Westbury train station.
It takes her 25 minutes to get from Bristol train station
to the Hippodrome.

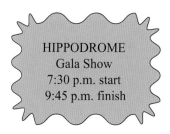

HIPPODROME
Gala Show
7:30 p.m. start
9:45 p.m. finish

(a) What is the latest time that she can leave home
so that she can get to the Hippodrome for
the start of the Gala Show?

(b) Natalia catches the earliest possible train after
the Gala Show back to Westbury. How long is it in
total between her leaving home and arriving back home?

* 9   In a Sports Club at 6 p.m.
last Tuesday there were 63 people
either in the Gym, playing
badminton or boxing.

A quarter of the 28 men were
boxing. Half of the 20 people
playing badminton were women.
There were 20 women in the Gym.

Find the total number of people
who were boxing.

* 10   Colin and eleven of his friends plan to have a game of golf then
a set meal. The prices are shown below:

Golf
£28 per person
15% off for groups
of 10 or more

Set meal
£15 per person
or £35 for every
3 people

Colin has £440 to pay for all the golf and the meals.
The money left over is to be given as a tip.
Work out how much the tip will be.

S | **STATISTICS 2**

* 1 Each week Lan has a Maths test and an English test.
The table below shows her marks (out of 20) for
each test during one half term.

	Week 1	Week 2	Week 3	Week 4	Week 5	Week 6
Maths	14	13	16	16	15	17
English	11	14	12	11	13	12

Lan wants to compare her Maths marks with her English marks.
On squared paper, draw a suitable diagram or chart.

* 2 240 students in Grafton School were asked which Harry Potter book
was their favourite. The results are shown in the first pie chart below.

The same question is given to 420 students in the Madeley High School.
The results are shown in the second pie chart below.

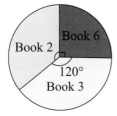   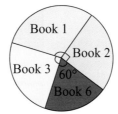

Grafton School   Madeley High School

In which school did more students prefer Book 2 and by how many?

* 3 86 children go on a watersports holiday.
One morning each child will waterski,
windsurf or dive.

11 out of the 40 girls go diving.

Half of the 28 children who waterski
are boys.

21 boys windsurf.

How many children go diving in total?

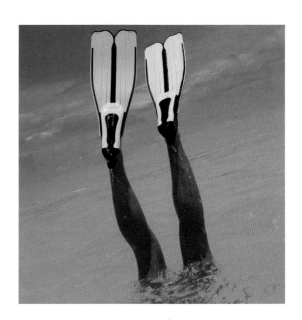

* 4   Luis has 3 cards each with a positive whole number written on it.

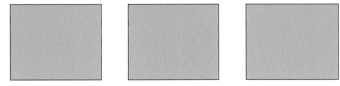

The median of the three numbers is 4.

The mean of the three numbers is 5.

(a) Work out the three numbers on the cards.

(b) There are four possible answers to part (a).

    Find all four possible sets of numbers.

* 5   Madelyn wants to find out how much time people spend watching the Olympics when the Games are being staged. She needs to design a questionnaire.
Make up a suitable question for Madelyn's questionnaire.

* 6   Thirteen people went out to collect money for the charity 'Food Aid'. Fifteen people collected money for the charity 'Save the Whales'. The total amount collected by each person is shown in the back-to-back stem and leaf diagram.

Food Aid			Save the Whales
9 3	2	4 6	
8 6 6	3	2 2 4 7 8	
5 2	4	1 6 9	
4 4 3	5	4	
1	6	7 8	
7 4	7	2 2	

Key 5|4 = £45   Key 4|6 = £46

The Food Aid people need to raise at least £600 to help a village in Africa.
Do they collect enough money? You must show all your working out.

* 7 Diego asked 40 people what their favourite food was.
His findings are shown in the table.

Type of meal	Frequency
Chinese	12
Indian	15
Italian	8
Thai	3
Other	2

Represent this information in
a suitable diagram or chart.

* 8 Ten people threw a dice.
Their scores are shown in the bar chart below.

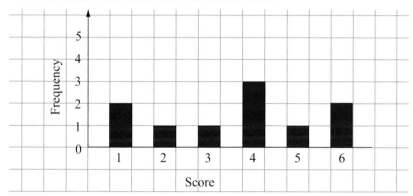

Calculate the mean score and the median score
(hint: write out the ten scores first).

* 9

In the list of six numbers above, the mode is 6 and
the range is 9. Calculate the mean for these six numbers.

* 10 Elena runs a grocer's store. One day she records
      how many of each type of fruit are sold.
      The information is shown below.

Type of fruit	Frequency
apple	302
banana	88
pear	162
pineapple	16
orange	124
melon	28

720 are sold in total. Represent
this information in a suitable
diagram or chart.

* 11 There is a 0.78 chance that an insurance claim made to
      the 'Magpie Insurance Company' will be a car claim.
      The car claim probability for the 'Denver Firm' is 0.6.

      During November the 'Magpie Insurance Company' receive 350
      insurance claims and the 'Denver Firm' receive 440 insurance claims.

      Which firm gets the most car claims and by how many?

* 12 A group of 27 people go to an adventure park.
      Their first ride is either on the Turbo Terror,
      the Curly Whirl or the Splashdown.
      Half of the 12 women go on
      the Turbo Terror. 5 men go on the
      Splashdown.

      10 people go on the Curly Whirl of
      whom $\frac{2}{5}$ are women.

      How many people in total go on
      the Splashdown first?

M   MIXED 5

* 1   Copy and complete this bill.

NORTON'S CHINA SHOP			
Number of items	Item	Cost of one item	Total
4	Cup	£8.50	£ _ _ _ _
5	Plate	£14.65	£73.25
3	Dish	£15.85	£ _ _ _ _
2	Bowl	£ _ _ _ _	£54.40
		Total	£ _ _ _ _
		VAT at 20%	£ _ _ _ _
		Total bill	£ _ _ _ _

* 2   Two groups of people were asked what
they were most frightened of.
The findings are shown below.

GROUP A   40 people
$\frac{1}{5}$ of the people said 'spiders'
$\frac{3}{8}$ of the people said 'rats'
The other people said 'closed spaces'

GROUP B   72 people
$\frac{1}{3}$ of the people said 'heights'
$\frac{2}{9}$ of the people said 'rats'
$\frac{1}{6}$ of the people said 'closed spaces'
The other people said 'spiders'

Find the total number of people
from both groups who said that
they were most frightened of
closed spaces?

* 3 Sixty people were asked
     what job they do.
     The findings are shown opposite.

Shop assistant 15

Nurse 18

Factory worker 12

     Represent this information in
     a suitable diagram or chart.

Postman 5

Plumber 5

Social worker 5

* 4 Milena sells candles at a market stall.

     One day she buys 45 boxes at £2.50 each.
     There are 16 candles in each box.

     She sells a box of candles for £3.50 or
     she sells individual candles at 60p each.

     By the end of the day she has sold
     35 boxes. She sells all the other candles
     individually but has 15 candles left over.

     How much profit does Milena
     make on the candles?

* 5

ARNDALE SAVINGS
4% per annum
compound interest

Ian invests £9000
in Arndale Savings.

Eva invests £6500
in Moxon Bank.

MOXON BANK
6% per annum
compound interest

Who gets the greater amount of interest after
two years and by how much?

* 6   Caroline wants to find out how much time
the members of the Dance group 'Mesmerise'
spend practising. She needs to design a questionnaire.

Make up a suitable question for Caroline's
questionnaire.

* 7

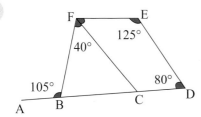

Calculate the size of angle CFE.

You must give reasons for each
step in your working.

* 8 Cooper's dog weighs 19.4 kg.
The amount of dog food from
a can to be eaten each day is shown below.

Weight of dog (kg)	Amount of food
Up to 11	$\frac{1}{4}$ can
11 to 20	$\frac{1}{3}$ can
20 to 30	$\frac{1}{2}$ can

Cooper buys the dog food from his local store.
The prices are shown in the table below.

1 can for 60p

3 cans for £1.70

6 cans for £3.20

Cooper wants to buy enough cans of dog food
for all the month of March. What is the least
amount of money he must spend? Explain
your answer fully.

* 9 The cost C of hiring a tile cutting machine is given by the formula

$$C = 23 + 15n$$

where n is the number of days of hire. How much more does it
cost to hire the machine for 9 days compared to 4 days?

* 10   Mr and Mrs Amos want to go to China on holiday.
A travel firm gives them the following prices. Each price
given is for one adult.

Departure date	7 nights	14 nights	21 nights
2 Sep – 16 Sep	£1425	£2065	£2490
17 Sep – 1 Oct	£1439	£2081	£2506
2 Oct – 23 Oct	£1461	£2110	£2524
24 Oct – 14 Nov	£1475	£2126	£2548
15 Nov – 5 Dec	£1489	£2153	£2573
6 Dec – 20 Dec	£1513	£2198	£2592
21 Dec – 4 Jan	£1528	£2215	£2605
5 Jan – 26 Jan	£1475	£2153	£2573
27 Jan – 17 Feb	£1439	£2081	£2506

The price is reduced for under 16 year-olds as follows:

    10% reduction on full price for 7 nights

    15% reduction on full price for 14 nights

    20% reduction on full price for 21 nights

Mr and Mrs Amos have 3 children
aged 9, 12 and 17. The whole family
wish to go to China for 14 nights,
leaving on 16th October.

Work out the cost of this holiday
from the information above.
Show all your working out.

Ⓜ **MIXED 6**

* 1 Most people have to pay a tax called National insurance.

Some workers have to pay 11% National insurance on all their earnings above £95 a week.

(a) During one week Jason earns £7.20 an hour and works for a total of 75 hours. How much will he pay in National insurance?

(b) During the same week Kaylee earns £7.40 an hour. She works for 80 hours plus 9 hours overtime. She is paid time and a half for any overtime work. How much will she pay in National insurance for that week? (Give your answer to the nearest penny)

* 2

SUNSHINE SHACK	
Soup of the day	£1.90
Pasty	£1.40
Toasted sandwich	£1.60
Salad	£1.50
Tea	80p
Coffee	90p
Juice	80p
Cola	70p

10% off all prices before 11 a.m.

Andrea and Claire arrive at the Sunshine Shack at 9:45 a.m. Andrea has soup and a cup of coffee. Claire has a toasted sandwich, a salad and a cup of tea.

Andrea pays for everything with a £10 note and leaves a £1 tip.
How much money does Andrea have left over from the £10 note?

* 3 Luka is fixing tiles onto the walls in his bathroom.
He uses 7 blue tiles for every 4 white tiles.
He uses two sizes of white tiles, large and small, in the ratio 1:5

Luka uses a total of 210 blue tiles.
How many small white tiles does he use?

* 4   The Taylor family are in the USA. The whole family want to spend
       2 hours swimming with dolphins at the Marine Centre in Florida.
       The prices are shown below.

THE MARINE CENTRE	
One hour swim with dolphins	
Adult	$54
Child	$39
Family ticket	$160
(2 adults and 2 children)	

The Taylor family consist of 2 adults and 4 children.

What is the least amount of money they will spend for their swim?

* 5   Payton drives from Glastonbury to Moreton-in-Marsh and back again.
       The reading on her speedometer before and after is shown below.

Before   57874   After   58060

Her car does 31 miles on one gallon of petrol. The cost of
petrol is shown below.

£6.98 per gallon

How much does it cost Payton to drive from Glastonbury to
Moreton-in-Marsh and back again?

44

* 6   Robert sells caravans for 'Harrison's caravans'.
He is paid £890 each month plus a bonus if
he sells more than 8 caravans as shown below.

> Bonus payment: £125 for each
> extra caravan sold above 8

Melanie sells caravans for 'Vanpark'.
She is paid £10320 per year. She also gets
a monthly bonus if she sells more than
9 caravans as shown opposite.

> Bonus:
>
> £100 for 1 extra sale above 9
> £300 for 2 extra sales above 9
> £550 for 3 extra sales above 9
> £850 for 4 extra sales above 9

(a) In April they both sell 12 caravans. Who earns more money
that month and by how much?

(b) In May they both sell 11 caravans. Does the same person
still earn more money? Explain your answer fully.

* 7

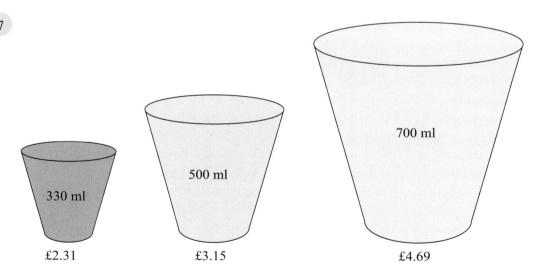

330 ml

£2.31

500 ml

£3.15

700 ml

£4.69

The prices of three different sized cups of cola at a cinema are shown above.

Which cup gives the *best value* for money? Explain your reasons fully.

* 8

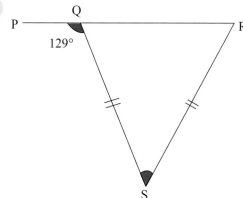

P Q R
129°

S

Triangle QRS is isosceles.

Work out the size of angle QSR.

You must give reasons for each step in your working.

* 9 Colton packs individual rings into boxes.

The number of rings he packs each hour during one day is shown below.

Time	Number of rings
9 am – 10 am	34
10 am – 11 am	42
11 am – 12 pm	48
12 pm – 1 pm	40
1 pm – 2 pm	0
2 pm – 3 pm	46
3 pm – 4 pm	44
4 pm – 5 pm	38
5 pm – 6 pm	25

Draw a suitable graph to show this information and suggest reasons why the number of rings are less between 1 pm and 2 pm as well as between 5 pm and 6 pm.

* **10** Arushi reads her gas meter at the start of September.
The dials below show the reading.

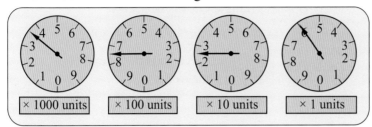

She reads the meter again at the start of December.
The dials below show the reading.

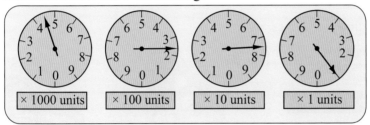

Arushi must pay 16.8p per unit for the first 220 units she has used.

She pays 12.4p per unit for the rest of the units she has used.

How much must she pay in total for this gas bill?

M | MIXED 7

* 1   Mr Reay is planning a school camp. For safety reasons there must be
one teacher for every ten students. 36 students go to the school camp.
The teachers do not pay to go to school camp.

The cost per person of one activity is shown opposite.

If all the students and teachers do one activity,
how much will each student need to pay to cover
the total cost?

Activity	
Climbing	
Canoeing	£18 per session
Caving	

* 2   Aidan needs to bake enough bakewell tarts for 53 people.
The recipe for the pastry is shown below.

Pastry (for 8 people)	
125 g	plain flour
75 g	butter
25 g	sugar
1	egg

The plain flour is sold in 500 g bags. How many bags must
Aidan buy to make all the bakewell tarts? Explain your working out fully.

* 3   There are 190 year 11 students in Heath Hill School.

82 of these students are female.

At the end of year 11 all the students will either stay
at school, go to college or leave education.
40 females go to college and 8 males leave education.
$\frac{3}{5}$ of the 80 students who stay at school are male.
Find the total number of students who go to college.

* 4 There are 72 flags flying outside a large building.
$\frac{5}{8}$ of these flags have blue in them.

Of these, $\frac{2}{3}$ also have red in them.

Of these, $\frac{1}{5}$ have green and $\frac{1}{2}$ have white.
How many flags in total contain blue, red, green or
blue, red, white?

* 5

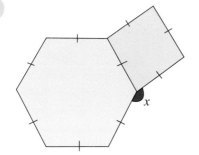

A square is attached to a regular
hexagon as shown.

Work out the value of angle x.

Explain your working out fully.

* 6 Mrs Collins needs to make a pack lunch for each of 60 children in her school.
She will include 2 bread rolls and one packet of crisps in each pack lunch.

Packets of crisps come in large packs of 8.

Bread rolls come in packs of 12.

Mrs Collins uses the least number of packs of everything.

How many bread rolls and packets of crisps will she have left over when
she has made all the lunches?

* 7 Grapefruit juice, blackcurrant juice and lemonade is mixed in the ratio 3:1:4 to make a juice cocktail.

(a) How much blackcurrant juice and lemonade is needed to make 16 litres of cocktail?

(b) Hunter needs 60 litres of drink for a party. He decides that one third of this will be juice cocktail. How much grapefruit juice will he need?

(c) What fraction of the cocktail is lemonade?

* 8 Lucy needs to hire a car for 3 months (13 weeks).

> 'Autohire' charge a fixed cost of £85 plus £21 for each day.

> 'Carmark' charge a fixed cost of £420 plus £118 for each week.

Which firm will be cheaper and by how much?

* 9

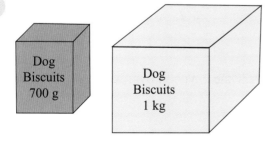

The small box of dog biscuits costs 98p.
The larger box costs £1.42

Which box is the better value?
Explain your answer fully.

* 10 The departure times of some trains from York to
      Birmingham New Street are shown below
      (Monday to Friday times).

York	0757	0830	0930	1057	1130	1157
Sheffield	0857	0930	1030	1157	1230	1257
Chesterfield	0921	0954	1054	1221	1254	1321
Derby	0943	1016	1116	1243	1316	1343
Burton	1016	1049	1149	1316	1349	1416
Birmingham New Street	1042	1115	1215	1342	1415	1442

Huan leaves a hotel in York at 0745. It takes her 20 minutes to get to
the train station.
She gets on the first possible train to Derby.

She gets off the train at Derby to do some shopping but must catch
a train to Birmingham New Street in time to meet
a friend there at 2:45 p.m.

What is the greatest amount of time that Huan can spend in Derby?

PART TWO

N | NUMBER 3

* 1   A shop is closing down and so it has a clearance sale.
The deal is shown below.

CLEARANCE SALE

$\frac{1}{3}$ off normal prices

plus an extra 20% off sale prices

Danielle buys a pair of shoes (normal price £108)
and a skirt (normal price £75).

How much will she pay in total in the sale?

* 2   Hannah buys a sketchpad for £12.50 to take on her holiday to Italy.
She fills up the pad in Rome so has to buy another sketchpad.
She pays 13.8 euros for her new sketchpad.

Is this cheaper or more
expensive than her first
sketchpad and by how much?
The exchange rate is
shown below.

£1 = 1.15 euros

* **3** Mr. and Mrs. Jenkins stay at the Melton hotel for a short holiday. They go on a Monday and stay for four nights in a double room.

They have evening dinner in the hotel on Monday and Wednesday only.

MELTON HOTEL	
	room cost per night
double room (Mon – Thu)	£130
double room (Fri – Sun)	£150
single room (Mon – Thu)	£105
single room (Fri – Sun)	£115
evening dinner £28.50 per person	

Mr. and Mrs. Jenkins get a 15% discount on the rooms only by booking the holiday through the Starlight Travel Company. How much do they pay in total for the room and evening dinners?

* **4** Carlos wants to build a wall. He needs to buy 480 bricks.
He finds three deals on the internet.

Deal 2

£17 for a box of 16 bricks

- - - - - - - - - - - -

Buy 5 boxes and get one extra box free

Deal 1

£26 for a box of 32 bricks

Deal 3

£70 for a box of 80 bricks

- - - - - - - - - - - -

10% discount on 5 or more boxes

Which deal will cost Carlos the least money?
Explain your reasons fully.

* 5   Chase sells computers. He has been promised a 12% pay increase if he sells at least 100 computers during the year. The increase will be 15% if he sells at least 120 computers during the year. The graph below shows his sales figures for the year. What will be his new salary if he earned £16200 during the current year?

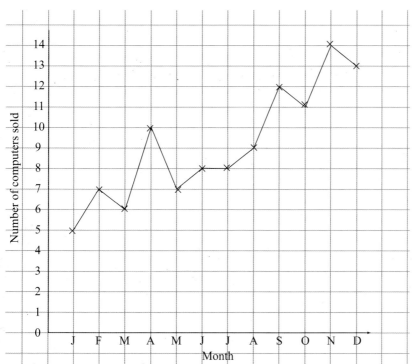

* 6   In a park there are 10 rabbits at the start of February.
Each month the number of rabbits doubles.
At the start of which month will the number of rabbits first be greater than 200?

* **7** Sophie goes to India for three weeks. She changes £750 into rupees. The exchange rate is shown below.

$$£1 = 75 \text{ rupees}$$

During her stay in India she spends 50340 rupees.

When Sophie returns home, she gives all the remaining money to her sister. Her sister needs £75 to see a music concert. Is Sophie's remaining money enough for this? Explain your answer fully.

* **8** Some theatre ticket prices are shown opposite.

Some friends go to see a show and spend a total of £172.30

If three of the friends bought Circle tickets, how many of them bought Stall tickets?

MERLIN THEATRE PRICES	
Stall	£26.20
Circle	£22.50

* **9**

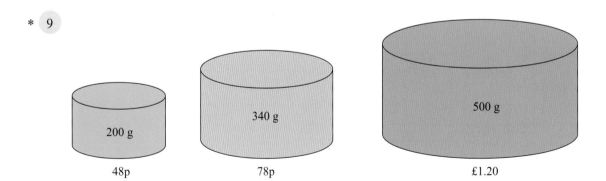

200 g   48p

340 g   78p

500 g   £1.20

The prices of three tins of baked beans are shown above.
Which tin gives the best value? Explain your answer fully.

* 10 The cost price and selling price of peppers in a local store are shown below.

Colour	Cost price	Selling price
Green	55p	80p
Yellow	40p	70p
Red	45p	75p

On Thursday the store manager buys 50 of each colour of pepper.

12 multipacks containing one pepper of each colour are sold for £1.90

The remaining peppers are sold individually.

At the end of the day the peppers shown below have not been sold.

Green	Yellow	Red	Multipack
2	5	3	4

Work out how much profit the store makes on the sale of peppers on that Thursday.
Show all your working out clearly.

Ⓜ MIXED 8

* 1   Alex wants to buy a camera. He tries the 3 shops below.

ELECTRO
Camera
£261
- - - - - - - - -
$\frac{1}{3}$ off
shown price

SHUTTER
Camera
£150
plus VAT
at 20%

MATSONS
Camera
Deposit £30
plus 12 monthly
payments of £11.50

Which shop offers Alex the cheapest deal?
Explain your reasons fully.

* 2   Food is served from a barbecue at a school fete.
The prices of the food and drink are shown below.

burger	£1.90	coke	80p
sausage	90p	lemonade	70p
kebab	£2.15	juice	75p
chicken	£1.85	water	70p
steak	£3.10		

(a) Gabrielle and her three friends turn up with a £10 note.
All the sausages have been sold. Have Gabrielle
and her friends got enough money for each of them
to have one item of food and one drink?
Explain your reasons fully.

(b) They actually borrow some money from
Gabrielle's mother and buy two kebabs, two steaks,
three cokes and one water. What is the least
amount of money they borrow from Gabrielle's mother?

* **3** Juan visits Chicago in the USA. His grandparents give him an extra £170 to spend. The graph below can be used to convert between £(pounds) and $(dollars).

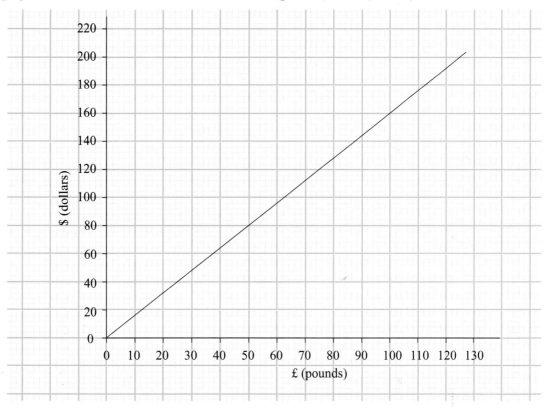

In Chicago Juan buys a jacket for $112, a baseball hat for $24 and a rucksack for $136.

How much money does he have left from his grandparents' money?

You must show all your working.

* **4** Maria wants to find out what topping people prefer on a pizza.

Design a data collection sheet that she can use to collect this information.

* 5

Tax allowance £8465

Income tax 20%

The tax allowance is the amount of money a person may earn before paying income tax on the remaining money.

A person pays 20% of the remaining money as income tax.

Huo earns £16000 for the year and Kevin earns £14500.

How much more income tax must Huo pay than Kevin?

* 6 Brooke went to her local ice skating centre.
She randomly asked 25 people for their ages.
These ages are shown in the stem and leaf diagram below.

```
0 | 7  8  8
1 | 2  5  5  6  6  7  9
2 | 1  2  2  4  7
3 | 2  4  5  5  9
4 | 3  6  6  7
5 | 2
```

Key 2|4 means 24 years old

(a) What was the probability that a person chosen would be more than 40 years old?

(b) There were a total of 100 people in the ice skating centre.
How many of these people were likely to have been more than 40 years old?

* 7

Type of food	Cost (week 1)	% change for week 2
Loaf of bread	£1.20	5% rise
Potatoes	64p per kg	stays same
Apples	85p per kg	20% drop
Pint of milk	50p	4% rise
Carrots	£1.40 per kg	5% drop
Bunch of 5 bananas	£1.10	stays same

In week 1 Vadim buys two loaves of bread,
5 kg of potatoes, 2 kg of apples, 3 pints of milk,
2 kg of carrots and 10 bananas.
He buys exactly the same amounts in week 2.
How much more or less does he spend in week 2?
Explain your working fully.

8

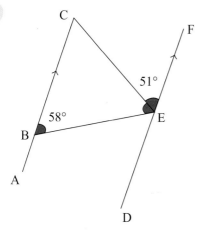

The lines AC and DF are parallel.
Calculate the value of angle BEC.
Give reasons for your answer.

* 9   Denver buys a caravan for £8000.

Each year it loses 10% of its value at the start of the year.

After two years Denver wants to buy a new caravan for £9000.
How much extra money will he need to find if he sells
his old caravan for its value after two years?

* 10   Leah makes ornaments from shells.

$\frac{2}{3}$ of the shells are used to make the outer
three rings.

The ratio of shells used in
the outer three rings is 9:11:15
moving from inside to outside.
If Leah uses 60 shells for
the outside ring, how many shells
does she use to make seven complete
ornaments?

Explain your working fully.

| N | **NUMBER 4** |

* 1 The exchange rates for Russia and
the USA are shown opposite.

£1 = 54.27 rubles
£1 = $1.58

The same type of hat can be bought in the UK, USA and Russia.
The standard price of the hat in each country is shown below.

UK	£17.69
USA	$28.44
Russia	922.59 rubles

In which country is the hat cheapest? Explain your answer fully.

* 2 Dylan and five friends want to watch
either motorcycle racing or go-karting.
The motorcycle racing costs £15.50
per person and is six miles from
Dylan's house. The go-karting costs
£12.50 per person and is nine miles
from Dylan's house. The local taxi
firm charges the following:

| Cab for four people | £2.70 per mile |
| Cab for nine people | £5.50 per mile |

Dylan and his friends wish to go by taxi. They choose the event which will
cost them the least money for entry to the event and a taxi there and back to
Dylan's house. How much cheaper per person is this choice?

* 3 In a supermarket, 'CLEANSE' dishwasher tablets are sold in
three sizes of box as shown below:

CLEANSE

56
tablets

£12.15

CLEANSE

28
tablets

£6.02

CLEANSE

14
tablets

£3.28

Which box is the best value for money? Show all your working out.

* **4** Some of the items produced each day in
a small factory are jars of carrots and peas.
The ratio of carrots to peas in each jar is 3:70.
A total of 288 carrots are used each day.
Each jar contains 280 peas.

How many jars of carrots and peas are produced
each day?

5 Layla spends $\frac{2}{3}$ of her time sleeping and working.

* She spends $\frac{1}{8}$ of her time on cooking and housework.

The rest of her time is spent on leisure.

What fraction of her time does Layla spend on leisure?

6 (a) Copy and complete the lower box for this phone bill.

*

Account number: SS 5372 1941

PHONE BILL TOTAL NOW DUE			
Cost of calls			
UK landline	Daytime	73 calls	£38.16
	Evening/weekend	136 calls	£29.14
To a mobile	Daytime	53 calls	£53.94
	Evening/weekend	69 calls	£38.26

Cost of calls	?
Line rental	£15.70
Total	?
VAT @ 20%	?
Due total	?

(b) The phone bill is paid in three equal monthly instalments.
Calculate the cost of one monthly instalment.

* 7 Shreya completes a Science exam which is made up of 3 sections.

Section A is worth 50 marks, section B is worth 30 marks and section C is worth 20 marks.

Shreya scores 32 marks on section A, $\frac{5}{6}$ of the marks for section B and 55% of the marks for section C.

What is Shreya's final total mark for this Science exam?

* 8 There is a major fire in Victoria in Australia. Planes are used to drop water on the fire. Plane A and plane B both leave their base at 08:00. Plane A returns to base every 50 minutes for more water and plane B returns to base every 70 minutes for more water. At what time will both planes next be back at their base together?

* 9

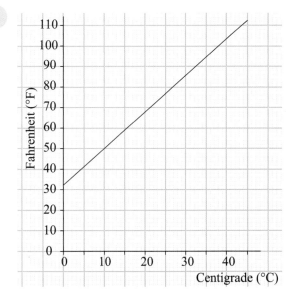

This graph can be used to convert degrees Fahrenheit into degrees Centigrade and vice versa.

Eric looks at five possible holiday destinations. He will not go to a place where the maximum temperature might go above 90 °F.

Write down which of the five places, in the table below, he will not go to on holiday.

Place	Maximum temperature
Barcelona	36° C
Lisbon	31° C
Nice	34° C
Venice	35° C
Belgrade	30° C

* 10 Simone's grandparents give her £40 to buy a shirt for her birthday. She decides to buy a shirt from a New York company in the USA. An import tax has to be paid to ship the shirt from the USA to the UK.

Using the figures below, how much money will Simone have left over from her grandparents' money? (Give your answer in pounds to the nearest penny)

Cost of shirt $40

import tax £11.50

Exchange rate £1 = $1.55

Ⓜ️ MIXED 9

* 1

CENTRAL GAS COMPANY
Previous reading 21784
Present reading 26159
@13.8p per unit of gas
Fixed quarterly charge £48.75

Hansen's furniture store receives its quarterly gas bill as shown opposite. Its monthly electricity bill is £107.62 Hansen's furniture store cannot allow its combined gas/electricity bills to exceed £1000 for this quarter (3 months). How much above or below £1000 are its combined gas/electricity bills?

* 2 Wyatt has four cards each with a number on it.

| 1 | | 2 | | 7 | | ? |

If the median of these four numbers is 2, what is the mean average for these four numbers?

* 3 It is the lambing season. There are 50 sheep in a field.

The ratio of the sheep who will have 0 lambs, 1 lamb, 2 lambs and 3 lambs is 4:3:2:1

Calculate the total number of lambs which these 50 sheep will have.

* 4 A shampoo manufacturer has made a new shampoo.
It wants to choose a name and so carries out a survey
to find out which name people prefer. The results are shown below.

Shampoo name	Number of men who prefer this name	Number of women who prefer this name
Hennas	70	140
Sokleen	30	110
Crème	120	50
Drizzle	280	60
Sunbeam	190	270
Marvel	40	110

Draw one or more suitable charts or diagrams to compare
what the men prefer to what the women prefer.
Which name should the manufacturer choose? Give your reasons.

* 5 At the start of the year in one part of
the Atlantic Ocean there are 3000 sealions
and 3000 dolphins. By the end of the year,
the population of sealions drops by 8% and
the number of dolphins rises by 3%.

What is the difference in the
number of sealions and the number
of dolphins by the end of the year?

* 6

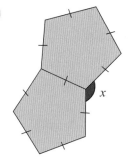

The diagram shows two regular pentagons
joined together. Calculate the value of angle x.
Explain your reasons fully.

* 7 The table opposite shows the exchange rates between the
UK and Mexico as well as the UK and the USA.

£1 = 21.25 pesos

£1 = $1.62

Katerina buys a jumper for $61.56 in the USA.
Mira buys the same jumper for 828.75 pesos in Mexico.

In which country was the jumper cheaper?
Show your full working out.

* 8

Flat A
1 bed. flat Colmers Farm, lge living room,
kitchen, bathroom, £95 p.w. including
electricity/gas, available immediately
Tel. 519732

Allison is looking for a flat.
She finds the details of two flats.

Flat B
1 bed. flat Saint Agnes, living
room/kitchen combined, £88 p.w.
plus electricity/gas to pay, shared
garden Tel. 678913

For flat A, Allison would need to take
two buses (each costing 80p) to get to
work and the same to get home again.
For flat B, Allison can get to work on
one bus only costing 70p and the same
to get home again.

Allison works from Monday to Friday each week. The average cost of
electricity would be £6.30 a week. The weekly average cost of gas would
be £5.50. By considering the rent, electricity, gas and bus travel, which
flat would be cheaper for Allison to take and by how much per week?

* 9 160 tourists to London are asked what their
favourite sights are. They all choose
Buckingham Palace, Tower Bridge,
Big Ben or the Tower of London.

10 of the 85 women choose Tower Bridge.

7 men choose Big Ben.

$\frac{3}{4}$ of the 60 people who choose the Tower of
London are men.

70% of the 70 people who choose
Buckingham Palace are women.

Find the total number of tourists
who choose Big Ben.

* 10 Jaxon earns £285 per week. The annual tax allowance is shown opposite.

Calculate how much money Jaxon has left per week when he has paid his income tax (assume 1 year = 52 weeks). Give your answer to the nearest penny.

Tax allowance = £8465

Tax rate 20%

A | ALGEBRA 1

* **1** The perimeter of the rectangular
room shown opposite is 36 m.

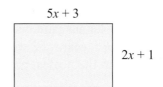

(a) Form an equation, in terms of x.

(b) Solve the equation to find the value of x.

(c) Find the actual area of this room (in m^2).

* **2** Copy the axes below.

Draw the graph of
$y = 2x + 5$ for values of x from $x = -4$ to $x = 3$.

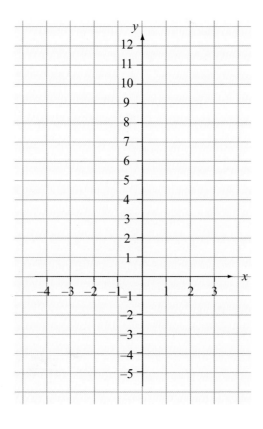

* 3 A school can buy boxes of pritt stick glue in two sizes.
A small box contains x sticks. A large box contains y sticks.

(a) The school buys 6 large boxes and 2 small boxes.
Write down an expression for the total number of sticks
the school buys.

(b) The school uses up $(2x + y)$ sticks. Write down an expression
for the number of sticks remaining.

(c) When the school bought 6 large boxes and 2 small boxes,
it had a total of 170 sticks. How many sticks might there
have been in each type of box?

* 4
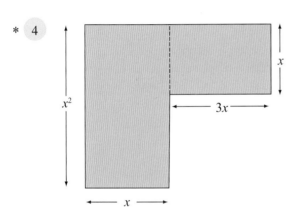

(a) Write down an expression, in terms of
x, for the total area of this L-shape.

(c) Calculate the actual area of this
L-shape when $x = 4$ cm.

* 5 A restaurant has a special price for more than
10 guests given by the formula below:

Price = fixed charge + £13 × number of guests

Calculate the number of guests if the fixed charge
was £55 and the guests paid a total of £315.

* 6

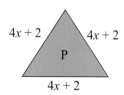

$4x + 2$ $4x + 2$

P

$4x + 2$

Q $x + 1$

$5x + 1$

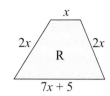

x

$2x$ $2x$

R

$7x + 5$

Which of the shapes above has the largest perimeter? Explain your answer fully.

* 7   Three friends have a total of 23 euro coins.
Max has x coins.

Zoe has twice as many coins as Max.

Lily has 5 coins less than Max.
How many coins does Lily have?

* 8   Copy the axes below.

Draw the graph of $y = x^2 + 3$ for
values of x from $x = -3$ to $x = 3$.

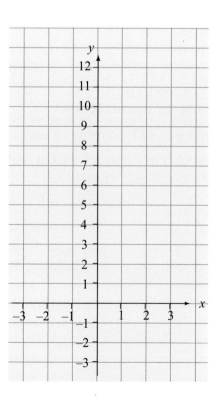

* ⑨ A young zebra weighs $(5a + 7b)$ kg.

During the following week it loses $(a + b)$ kg of its weight.

In the week after that it gains $(2a + 3b)$ kg in weight.

Write down an expression for what the zebra now weighs.

* ⑩

3x + 2

x ▮ x

4x − 3

Work out the actual perimeter of this rectangle.
All measurements are given in cm. (hint: opposite sides of a rectangle are equal)

M	MIXED 10

* 1   The table opposite shows the price of an XIV dishwasher at the end of each year shown.

Cameron buys an XIV dishwasher at the end of 2008.

Year	Price
2007	£742
2008	£762
2009	£787
2010	£814
2011	£838

He pays £4.54 each month insurance for repairs to his dishwasher or help towards buying a new dishwasher.

During	Percentage of new dishwasher
Year 1	100%
Year 2	80%
Year 3	60%
Year 4	40%
Year 5	20%

If his dishwasher cannot be mended, the insurance will pay a percentage of the cost of a new dishwasher as shown in the table opposite.

Cameron's dishwasher breaks down at the end of 2011.
He has to buy a new XIV dishwasher.

(a) How much money for the new dishwasher is paid from the insurance?

(b) Has Cameron saved money overall by making monthly insurance payments?
    If so, how much money has he saved?

* 2

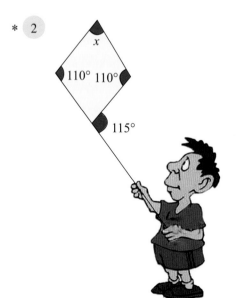

Calculate the angle x at the top of Joe's kite.
Explain your working fully.

* 3   The Howell family are going on a ski holiday.
They need to hire skis and jackets and must also buy ski passes.
The prices in three resort shops are shown below.

Shop A	
Ski hire	€15 per day
Ski hire (under 16)	€12 per day
jacket	€3.50 per day
ski pass	€20 per day
	or €35 for every 2 days

Shop B	
Ski hire	€90 per week
Ski hire (under 16)	€70 per week
jacket	€26 per week
ski pass	€130 per week

Mr and Mrs Howell have
two children, aged 9 and 12.

Explain the cheapest way in which the
Howell family can all hire skis,
a jacket and buy a ski pass for
a seven day holiday.

Give the total number of euros
they must spend.

Shop C	
Ski hire	€18 per day
	or €44 for every 3 days
Ski hire (under 16)	€12 per day
	or €30 for every 3 days
jacket	€3.50 per day
	or €10 for every 3 days
ski pass	€20 per day
	or €56 for every 3 days

* 4   The exchange rates in London and
Berlin one day are shown opposite.

Evelyn is travelling from London
to Berlin. She has £800 to change
into euros (€). Will she get more euros in
London or Berlin? How many more euros will she get?

London £1 = €1.16
Berlin €1 = 87p

* 5 Throughout her early life, Savannah is given many cuddly toys when it is her birthday. She keeps all her cuddly toys.

The table below shows how many cuddly toys she has in total when she reaches each birthday.

Birthday	1	2	3	4	5	6	7
Number of cuddly toys	3	5	8	12	17		

(a) The above pattern continues. How many cuddly toys will she have on birthday 6?

(b) On which birthday will she have a total of 47 cuddly toys?

* 6

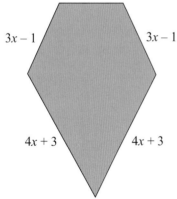

2x

3x − 1   3x − 1

4x + 3   4x + 3

The perimeter of this pentagon is 52 cm.

What is the actual length of the longest side of this pentagon?

Give your answer in cm.

* 7 45 people were asked what their favourite
  athletics track event was.
  The results are shown in the table below.

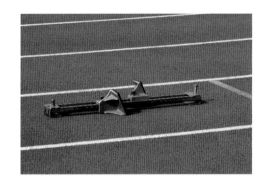

Event	Number of people
100 m	16
200 m	5
400 m	5
800 m	3
1500 m	12
5000 m	4

Represent this information in a suitable diagram or chart.

* 8 Bread rolls are sold in packs as shown below.

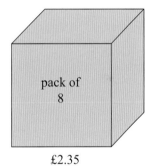

pack of 2   pack of 4   pack of 8

66p   £1.20   £2.35

Mrs Ryall has to make rolls for a party on Friday then for another party
on Saturday. The bread rolls do not stay fresh overnight so she can only
buy them on the day of the party.

Describe the cheapest way of buying the bread rolls if she needs 39 on
the Friday and 29 on the Saturday.

* 9 Copy the axes opposite. Draw the graph of
$y = 3x - 1$ for values of x from $x = -2$ to $x = 4$.

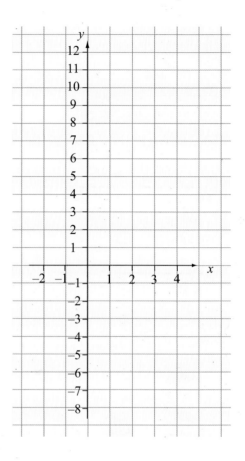

* 10 Molly has £1400 for a fortnight's holiday in Egypt.
She looks on the internet and finds the information below.

Flights	
From Manchester to Cairo (Egypt)	From Cairo to Manchester
6:20 am £270	10:15 pm £235
9:45 am £440	1:05 pm £79

Hotels: rate per night	
2*	£55
3*	£75
4*	£95
5*	£125

Molly needs to fly from Manchester but will not fly at night. She does not want to stay in a basic 2* hotel. Molly must stay within her budget.

Which flights and hotels can she choose?

You must write down all your calculations clearly to show that Molly is within her budget.

GEOMETRY 2

* 1

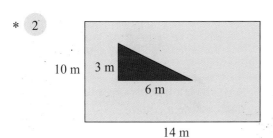

7 cm

10 cm

12 cm

Parker covers this box with wrapping paper. He uses an extra 90 cm² of wrapping paper for overlaps.

What area of wrapping paper will he have left from a square sheet measuring 50 cm × 50 cm?

* 2

10 m 3 m

6 m

14 m

Maria has a rectangular garden with a triangular flower bed as shown.

Apart from the flower bed, Maria wants to turf the rest of the garden. Turf costs £3.25 per square metre.

How much will it cost Maria to lay turf in her garden?

* 3 Calculate the value of angle x.

Show your working out clearly.

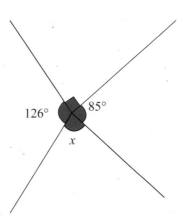

126° 85°

x

78

* 4   The cardboard box opposite measures
100 cm × 75 cm × 55 cm.

Julian has 80 packets with the dimensions
25 cm × 25 cm × 10 cm.

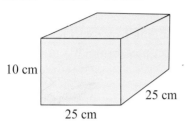

Julian puts as many packets as possible into
the cardboard box and seals it.

How many packets are left over?

* 5

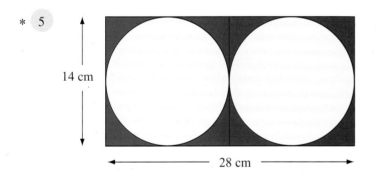

This diagram shows two circles,
each inside a square.

Calculate the red area.
(Give your answer to one decimal
place.)

* 6   This plan is the living room in Vicky's house.
There are two doors, each 0.5 m wide.

Vicky wants to put skirting board all around
the bottom of each wall.

The cost of the skirting board is shown below.
VAT needs to be added to each item at 20%.

1m length	£3
pack of four 1m lengths	£11.50
pack of four 2m lengths	£19

What is the least amount of money
Vicky must pay for the skirting board
for her living room?

* 7

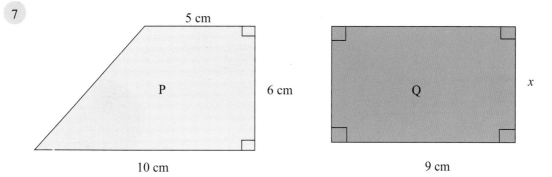

5 cm

P

6 cm

Q

x

10 cm

9 cm

Find the length x if the area of shape P is
equal to the area of shape Q.

* 8   A shop sells rolls of carpets which are wide enough
for Eric's rectangular bedroom. The carpet can be
bought in lengths as shown in the table opposite.

Eric measures the length of his bedroom as 11 feet.
He must convert this into metres to decide
which length of carpet to buy.

Carpet length	Cost
2.5 m	£128
3 m	£153.60
3.5 m	£179.20
4 m	£204.80
4.5 m	£230.40
5 m	£256
5.5 m	£281.60
6 m	£307.20

Using the information shown opposite,
what is the least amount of money
Eric can spend to carpet his bedroom?

1 inch = 2.5 cm

1 foot = 12 inches

1 kg   = 2.2 pounds

1 litre = 1.8 pints

* 9

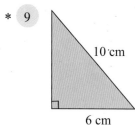

10 cm

Calculate the area of this triangle.

6 cm

* 10

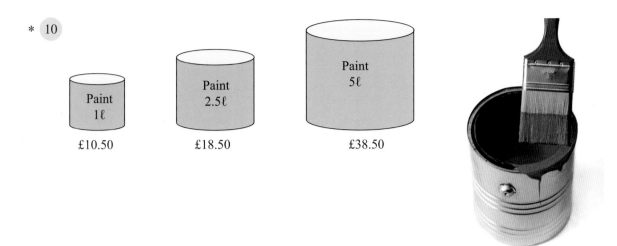

Paint
1ℓ

£10.50

Paint
2.5ℓ

£18.50

Paint
5ℓ

£38.50

Makayla wants to paint 3 walls in a room as shown below.

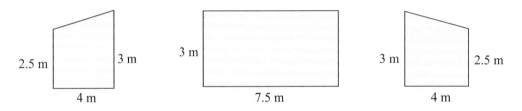

2.5 m   3 m
   4 m

3 m
   7.5 m

3 m   2.5 m
   4 m

If 1 litre of paint will cover an area of 6 m², which tins of paint must
Makayla buy so that she pays the least amount of money?
Give full reasons for your answer.

MIXED 11

* 1   Mrs Reece organizes a year 11 trip to the theatre to see
a play for their GCSE English. The costs are shown below:

ticket	£12.50 (buy 9 tickets and get one extra ticket free)
coach (52 seats)	£325
other costs	£35

Each student has to pay £19.

90 students go on the trip.

(a) How much money is left over when all the costs have been paid?

(b) At the last minute the theatre removes its free ticket offer.
Is there still enough money to cover the costs?
If not, how much more money is needed?

* 2   The distances (in km) between several towns is shown below.

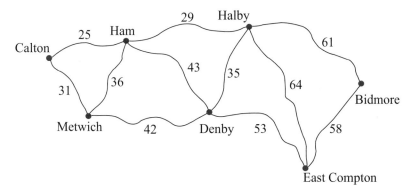

All the towns need to be connected to each other by a TV cable.
Copy the diagram then work out the least amount of
TV cable that would be needed. Explain your answer fully.

* ③ Anna has *x* coloured pencils.
Charles has four times as many
pencils as Anna.

Bailey has 3 more
pencils than Charles.

They have a total of 30 pencils.
How many pencils does
Bailey have?

* ④ Tom is a student. He lives on a total of £7500 for the year.
45% of the money comes from a student loan.
His parents give him 30% of the money.

He earns the rest of the money by delivering papers
and doing bar work in the ratio 9:16.

How much money does he earn from the bar work?

* ⑤ Simon works on a building site. He is paid £8.80
per hour for an 8 hour day. He is paid time and a half
for working any hours above 8 hours.

On Monday he worked on four houses for the times
shown below.

House A: 2 hours 20 minutes

House B: 3 hours 45 minutes

House C: 50 minutes

House D: 2 hours 35 minutes

How much money does Simon earn on Monday?

* 6 The table below shows how many main meals
were sold during one week in two Indian restaurants.

	Monday	Tuesday	Wednesday	Thursday	Friday	Saturday	Sunday
The Rajah	10	14	26	30	58	60	28
Spice House	22	28	30	28	32	36	20

Claire wants to compare the number of main meals sold in
the Rajah with the number of main meals sold in the Spice House.

On squared paper, draw a suitable chart or diagram she could use.

* 7 During one evening a restaurant makes and
sells 10.5 litres of coffee.

250 ml of coffee is used for each cup.

One cup of coffee costs £2.30

Find the total amount of money the restaurant
receives for selling coffee during that evening.

* 8 Riley travels 14 miles in 15 minutes. She drives at
this steady speed for 2 hours from Durham to Sheffield.

The distances from Durham to Sheffield and from
Sheffield to London are in the ratio 2:3.
What is the distance from Sheffield to London?

* 9

A window cleaner leans a ladder against a wall.

The bottom of the ladder is 1.65 m from the wall.

The top of the ladder reaches up to the bottom of a window which is 3.96 m above the ground.

Work out the length of the ladder.

* 10   Bryan lives in Wells. He wants to meet a friend in Bath for a pizza.
He needs to travel by bus. The bus timetable is shown below.

173: Wells – Bath										
Sevice No.:	**173**	**173**	**173**	**173**	**173**	**173**	**173**	**173**	**173**	**173**
Wells Bus Station	0655	0750	0943	1043	1143	1243	1343	1443	1543	1643
Gurney Slade	0715	0810	1003	1103	1203	1303	1403	1503	1603	1703
Chilcompton	0721	0816	1009	1109	1209	1309	1409	1509	1609	1709
Radstock	0743	0839	1031	1131	1231	1331	1431	1531	1631	1731
Dunkerton	0756	0853	1044	1144	1244	1344	1444	1544	1644	1744
Bath, Bus Station	0812	0909	1100	1200	1300	1400	1500	1600	1700	1800
173: Bath – Wells										
Bath, Bus Station	– – –	0910	1010	1110	1210	1310	1410	1510	1610	1710
Dunkerton	– – –	0924	1024	1124	1224	1324	1424	1524	1624	1724
Radstock	– – –	0940	1040	1140	1240	1340	1440	1540	1640	1740
Chilcompton	0756	0957	1057	1157	1257	1357	1457	1557	1657	1757
Gurney Slade	0806	1007	1107	1207	1307	1407	1507	1607	1707	1807
Wells Bus Station	0826	1027	1127	1227	1327	1427	1527	1627	1727	1827

It takes Bryan 20 minutes to walk from his home to Wells Bus Station.

It takes him 15 minutes to walk from Bath Bus Station to the pizza restaurant.
He has arranged to meet his friend at Bath Bus Station at 1:10 pm.

They spend $1\frac{1}{2}$ hours at the pizza restaurant. Bryan then heads straight back to the bus station and catches the first possible bus home. He then walks directly back to his house.

At what time should Bryan arrive back home?

GEOMETRY 3

* 1 Each white circle in this photo has radius 5 cm. The whole shape is a rectangle of length 1 metre and width 68 cm.

Calculate the black area. Give the answer to the nearest whole number in cm^2.

* 2

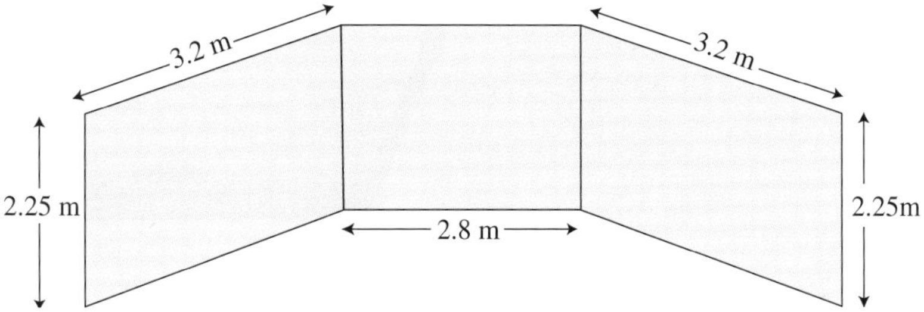

Uma wants to title three walls in her kitchen.

One wall is a rectangle of length 2.8 m and width 2.25 m. The other two walls are each of length 3.2 m and width 2.25 m.

Each rectangular tile has length 25 cm and width 20 cm.

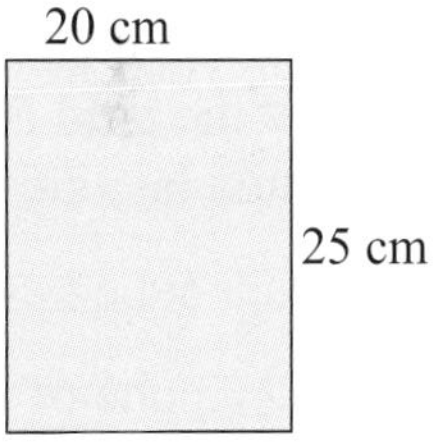

Uma can buy the tiles in boxes of 30. She buys one extra box to allow for mistakes when tiling.
Each box of tiles costs £31.20.

How much does Uma pay for all the tiles?

* 3

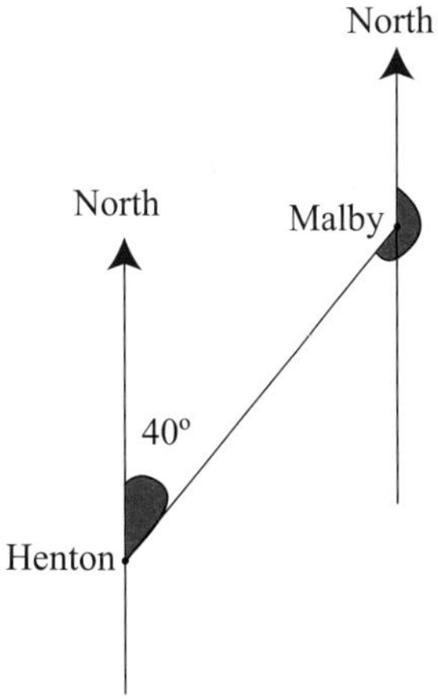

The bearing of Malby from Henton is 040°.
Work out the bearing of Henton from Malby as shown.

* 4   Oliver has a square garden. The area of the garden is 121 m².

Oliver's house borders one side of the garden. The rest of the garden has fencing around the edge apart from a 1.5 m wide gate.

What is the total length of fencing used for his garden?

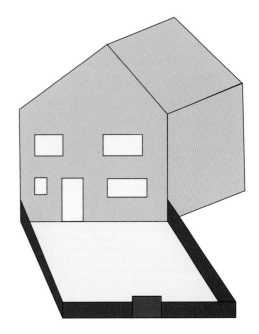

* 5   Each bar of gold measures 18 cm × 7 cm × 6 cm. There are 36 bars of gold.

All the gold is melted down and made into cubes.

Each cube has side length 3 cm.

Each cube of gold is worth £30000.

Calculate the total value of all the gold.

* 6

ACDF is a rectangle.

Lines BF and CE are parallel.

Work out the value of angle BCE.

You must give reasons to explain your answer.

* 7

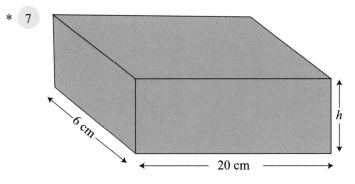

This cuboid has volume 480 cm³.

It has length 20 cm, width 6 cm and height *h* cm.

Work out the total surface area of the cuboid.

Give the answer in cm².

* 8

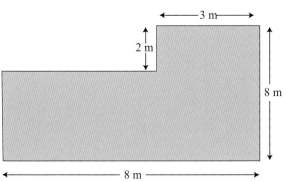

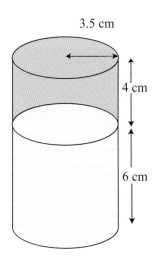

Ayden wants to carpet the room shown above. Any carpet he buys will be 6 m wide. He only wants one line where two pieces of carpet join together. The carpet costs £25 per square metre.

What is the least amount Ayden will have to spend to carpet the entire room? Explain your working out fully.

* 9 A glass in the shape of a cylinder has radius 3.5 cm. It is filled with lemonade to a height of 6 cm.

Carly's parents fill 50 glasses in this way for a party.

They buy the lemonade in one litre bottles.

How many bottles of lemonade do they need?

(Reminder: 1 litre = 1000 cm³)

* 10

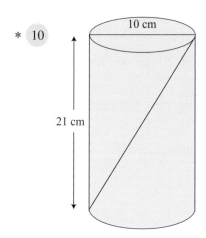

A pencil case is in the shape of a cylinder.

Its length is 21 cm and its diameter is 10 cm.

Can a pencil of length 23 cm fit inside this pencil case?

You must show all your working out.

MIXED 12

* 1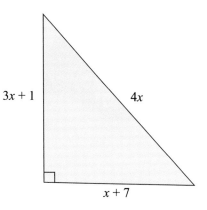

$3x + 1$ $4x$

$x + 7$

The perimeter of this triangle is 48 cm.

Work out the actual area of the triangle in cm².

* 2 Copy the axes below.

Draw the graph of $y = x^2 + 2$ for values of x from $x = -4$ to $x = 4$.

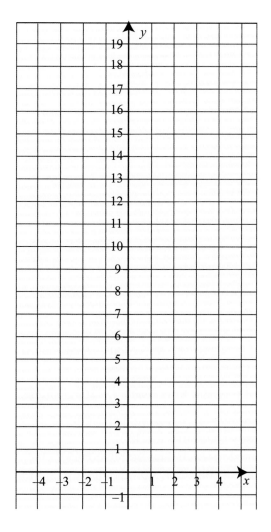

* 3 Renata parks her car in a city
    supermarket car park.

    The first $1\frac{1}{2}$ hours is free of charge.

    After that, Renata has to pay 60p for
    every 20 minutes or part of 20 minutes.

    How much does Renata pay if she arrives
    at 1:15 pm and leaves the car park
    at 4:30 pm?

* 4 Kate walked from her home to her grandparents' home, a total distance of 14 km.
    On her way she stopped for 30 minutes at a shop.

    The first part of her journey is shown in the travel graph below.

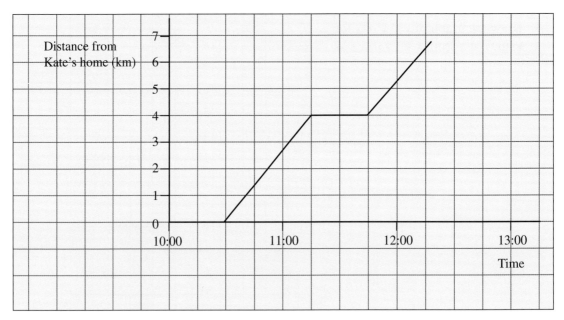

    From 11:45 onwards she walked at a steady speed until
    she reached her grandparents' home.

    (a) At what time did Kate reach her grandparents' home?

    (b) Kate's brother cycled from their home to their grandparents' home
         at a steady speed of 7 km/h.
         He wanted to reach their grandparents' home at exactly the same time as Kate.
         At what time did Kate's brother have to start his journey?

* 5   Hayley makes four window frames for a new house. For each window frame she needs three pieces of wood which are 1.2 m long and three pieces of wood which are 1 m long.

The wood is delivered to Hayley in lengths of 3.5 m.

What is the least number of 3.5 m lengths of wood that Hayley will have to cut to make her four window frames? Explain fully how she would get the pieces of wood that she needs.

* 6

Item	Weight
Bag of sugar	500 g
Apples	820 g
Bag of plain flour	1 kg
Cheese	370 g
Potatoes	4.2 kg
Carrots	585 g

Sinead has a very painful back. Her doctor has told her that she must not carry more than 7.5 kg of items.

Can Sinead safely carry all her shopping shown in the table opposite?

Explain your answer fully.

* 7

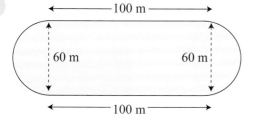

The diagram above shows a running track made from a rectangle and two semi-circles.

An athlete runs completely around the track four times. Work out the total distance the athlete runs. Give the answer to the nearest metre.

* 8 Ken uses his van to transport furniture. He moves some furniture for
     Mrs. Thomas and gives her the bill shown below.

Kenny Move			
Mrs. Thomas 5, Wayside Leeds LS10 5BM	Job number 312		
10th March **number of units**	**Price per unit**	**Total**	**VAT (20%)**
2 tables	£15	£30	£6
4 chairs	£6	£24	£5.20
1 bed	£20	£20	£4
1 wardrobe	£18	£18	£3.60
	Total	£92 +	£18.80
		To pay	£110.80

Mrs Thomas spots a mistake on the bill.
What mistake has been made and what should be the total to pay?

* 9 Anya has £35 to spend on petrol and a car wash.

     Her car travels 9 miles for every one litre of petrol.

     > Petrol price   £1.49 per litre

     Anya must put enough petrol into her car to travel 180 miles.
     What is the most expensive car wash setting she can afford
     from the list below after she has paid for her petrol?
     You must show all your working out.

CAR WASH	
Wash	£4.20
Wash including 4 wheel scrub	£4.80
Wash and dry, including 4 wheel scrub	£5.50
Full wash and wax shine	£6.50

* 10 Edward plans to wallpaper two complete walls in his living room. Each wall is 2.5 m high and a plan of the living room is shown opposite.

A wallpaper roll is 8 m long and 80 cm wide.

Each roll of wallpaper costs £18.50

How many rolls of wallpaper will Edward need and what will be the total cost?

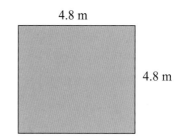

4.8 m

4.8 m

S | STATISTICS 3

* 1 A shoe shop records the heights and shoe sizes of a number of people.

The information is shown on the scatter graph below.

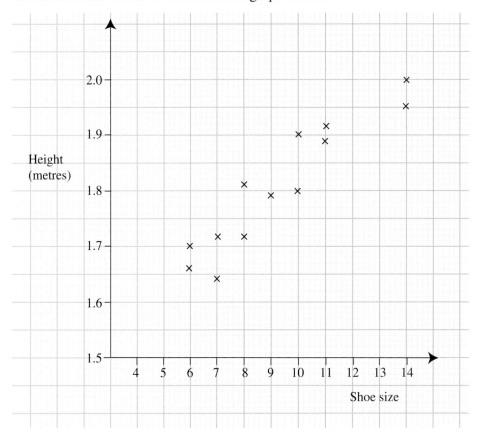

One more person of height 1.82 m has shoe size 11.

(a) Copy the scatter graph and mark on this final person.

(b) Describe the relationship between the shoe sizes and the heights of these people.

(c) Estimate the height of a person with shoe size 12.

* 2 A grocer measured the lengths of 16
bananas in one box (box A).
Each length is given below to
the nearest cm.

21   18   22   22   19   17   20   21

17   22   20   18   17   21   17   21

(a) Copy and complete the frequency
table for these bananas.

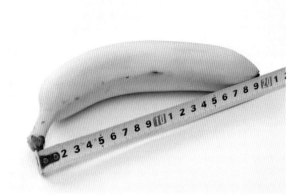

Length (cm)	Tally	Frequency
17		
18		
19		
20		
21		
22		

(b) Write down the mode, median and range of
the length of the bananas.

(c) The grocer measures the lengths of some bananas
from another box (box B).

He works out the following:

mode = 16 cm   mean = 17.8 cm

median = 17 cm   range = 10 cm

Compare the lengths of the bananas in box A with the lengths of
the bananas in box B. (Hint: use an average and the range)

* 3 Amelia wants to find out what the
favourite pet is for each student in
her class.

Design a suitable data collection sheet
she could use to collect this **information**.

* 4   During one week Ian and Julia take tests in five subjects.
Their test marks are shown below.

	English	Maths	Science	French	History
Ian	7	6	9	5	6
Julia	9	9	7	8	9

Their form tutor wants to compare their tests marks.

On squared paper, draw a suitable chart or diagram their form tutor could use.

* 5   A headteacher meets ten parents during one day,
shaking their hand when greeting them.

The length of time when shaking hands with each
parent is shown below.

Length of handshake (seconds)	Frequency
1	5
2	4
3	1

Work out the median length of handshake and the range for the lengths of handshake.
(Hint: List the ten handshakes in order of length, smallest first)

* 6 A certain make of car cost £11500 when it was brand new.
The values of some cars of this make are recorded in the years that follow.

The values are shown on the scatter graph below.

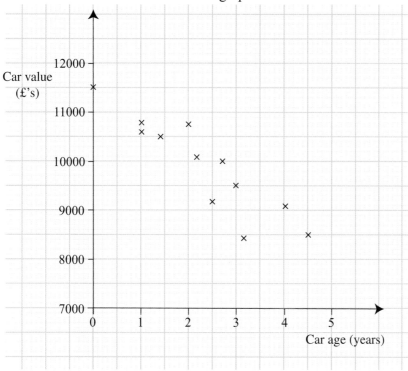

(a) Describe the relationship between the car value and the car age.

(b) Copy the scatter graph then estimate the value of a car which is 3.5 years old.

* 7 90 people were asked how they mostly exercise.
They all said that they cycle, jog or go to the gym.

55 of the people were over 30 years old and seven
of them chose 'jog'.

80% of the 50 people who chose 'gym' were over
30 years old.

20 people who chose 'cycle' were 30 years old or under.

How many people in total said they prefer to cycle?

98

* 8　An airport records the number of cases each passenger has.
The results for the first 50 passengers are shown below:

2 1 1 3 1 0 2 2 1 3 3 0 1 1 0 1 2 3 4 2 1 3 1 1 2

3 1 0 0 2 2 2 1 0 3 1 1 2 0 1 1 1 2 1 4 0 1 1 2 2

(a) Copy and complete the frequency table.

(b) Calculate the total number of cases brought by these 50 passengers.

(c) Find the mean number of cases per passenger.

Number of cases	Frequency
0	
1	
2	
3	
4	

* 9　Murray throws a dice 40 times. His scores are shown in the frequency table below.

Score	Frequency
1	10
2	8
3	6
4	7
5	7
6	2

Calculate Murray's mean score.

* 10　Kevin has 13 innings in cricket and makes the scores shown below.

8　82　17　51　39　6　12　42　37　68　19　46　58

(a) Find his median score.

(b) Find the range of his scores.

(c) James has 17 innings. His scores are shown in the stem and leaf diagram below.

```
1 | 9
2 | 1 3 3
3 | 2 5
4 | 6
5 | 4 7 7 9
6 | 1 2 2 5 8
7 | 2
```

Key 4|6 means 46 runs

Use the median and range to compare the scores for Kevin with the scores for James.

M MIXED 13

* 1 Hamish wants to invest £5000 for two years. Three banks offer the following deals.

EASY BANK
Fixed rate 4% per annum Compound interest

TRICKIER BANK
1st year : 3% per annum 2nd year: 5% per annum

MAYBE BANK
Fixed rate 3% per annum compound interest plus bonus of £100 at the end of 2 years

Which bank should Hamish use to make the most money? Show your full working out.

* 2 The times of some Saturday evening programmes are shown below.

19:05	Doctor Who
19:55	In it to win it
20:45	Casualty
21:40	Outnumbered
22:10	News
22:25	Match of the Day

Jess records Doctor Who, Casualty and Outnumbered.

She starts watching the programmes at 14:15 on Sunday.

She watches all the programmes in one go.

At what time on Sunday does the last programme finish?

* 3

Chocolates 4.14 euros 250 g

Exchange rate £1 = 1.15 euros

Maurice is in Bruges and buys
the Belgium chocolates shown opposite.

When he gets back to England,
he finds $\frac{1}{2}$ kg of the same type of
chocolates being sold for £7.76

In which country were the chocolates
better value for money, Belgium or England?
Show all your working out.

* 4 Mrs Parker wants three sides of her house to be painted. Painter, Carl, offers to do the whole job for £450. Another painter, Helen, offers to do the job for £3 per square metre.

The three sides of the house to be painted are shown below. Each window has area 2m². Each door has area 2.5 m².

Who should Mrs Parker choose to paint her house so that she spends the least amount of money? How much cheaper is this painter?

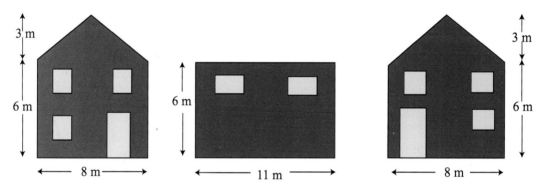

* 5

Flavour	Number put on shelf	Number left on shelf
Plain	110	42
Cheese and onion	130	24
Roast chicken	60	9

The manager of a garage is given a target that each week the garage must sell at least $\frac{2}{3}$ of the packets of crisps which are put on the shelf.

The table above shows how many packets of crisps were put on the shelf during one week and how many were not sold.

Did the garage meet the target? Explain your answer fully.

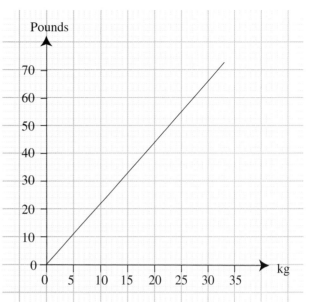

* 6 Holly has 3 dogs, weighing
     28 pounds, 20 pounds and 34 pounds.

     She has to buy 'worming' packets
     for each dog.
     They are sold in the sizes shown below.

     Use the graph opposite to work out
     which packets Holly must buy and
     what the total cost will be.

Worming treatment for dogs of size 5 kg – 10 kg	Worming treatment for dogs of size 10 kg – 20 kg	Worming treatment for dogs of size over 20 kg
£32	£39	£45

* 7 Chloe, Jose and Ashna play games of
     pool against each other.

     Chloe pots x balls.

     Jose pots twice as many balls as Chloe.

     Ashna pots six more balls than Chloe.

     They pot a total of 74 balls.

     How many balls did Chloe pot?

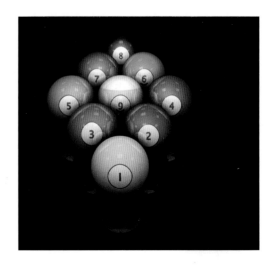

* 8 Lillian earns £1382.50 each month. Her income tax allowance and
     the tax rate are shown below.

Tax allowance per year	£9120

Tax rate	20%

How much income tax does Lillian have to pay each month?

* 9 Nathan and his friends sell raffle tickets to raise
     money for charity. Each ticket costs 50p.

They raise £621 when the raffle is made and they
have paid for the prizes shown below.

Balloon ride for two	£90
Restaurant meal for two	£50
Two local theatre tickets	£32
Bottle of Bordeaux wine	£15

How many raffle tickets did Nathan and his friends
sell in total?

* 10 Kylie is designing a paper weight as shown below. Blue objects
     A and B are made from the same material and must weigh
     the same amount. What length x should object B be made by Kylie?

4 cm A 2 cm
          4 cm 3 cm

3 cm B
      3 cm x

S | STATISTICS 4

* 1   Blake and Stella play a game of darts.
Their scores with each
set of three darts is shown below.

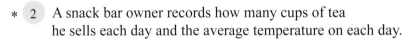

Blake: 40 27 8   78 55 58
        60 60 52 23 40

Stella: 26 41 60 60 37
       29 52 39 34 58

Compare fully the scores for Blake and Stella.

* 2   A snack bar owner records how many cups of tea
he sells each day and the average temperature on each day.

The information is shown on the scatter graph below.

The average temperature on one other day is 9.6° C when
he sells 40 cups of tea.

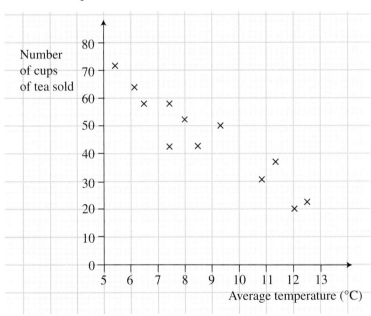

(a) Copy the scatter graph and mark a final point using the information above.

(b) Describe the relationship between the average temperature and
the number of cups of tea sold.

(c) Estimate the number of cups of tea which will be sold if
the average temperature is 10° C.

* **3** Twenty five children take a times table test. Their test marks are shown in the chart below.

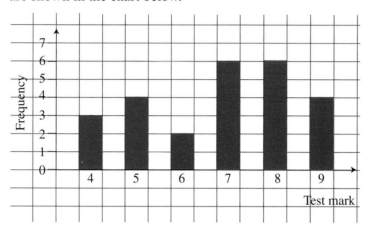

Calculate the mean test mark for these 25 children.

* **4** A hairdresser records how long people's appointments take during the month of February. The information is shown below.

Time (to nearest minute)	0 to 15	16 to 20	21 to 25	26 to 30	over 30
Number of people	32	42	124	73	29

(a) What is the probability that a person with a hair appointment would need 16 to 20 minutes?

(b) 500 people come to the hairdresser during March. How many of these people would you expect to need 16 to 20 minutes?

* **5** Louise wants to find out how often people eat ice cream. She will use a questionnaire.

Design a suitable question for Louise's questionnaire.

* 6 The times of sprinters in two 200 m races are recorded.
The results are shown in the back-to-back stem and leaf diagram.

	Race A					Race B					
				21		8	9				
	8	7	5	22		2	2	4	7	8	9
9	6	4	2	23		1					
			3	24							

Key 7|22 means 22.7 seconds   Key 22|8 means 22.8 seconds

Compare fully the times taken in race A with the times taken in race B.

* 7 90 people are asked what their
favourite form of transport is.
The information is shown in
the table below.

Form of transport	Frequency
Car	8
Boat	20
Plane	14
Bike	16
Train	25
Other	7

Represent this information in a suitable diagram or chart.

* 8 A group of students are given a Science exam and a Maths exam.

Their results are shown on the scatter graph below.

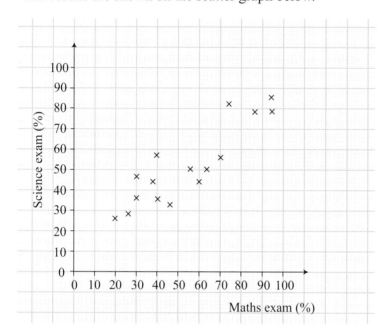

One more student scored 58% for Maths and 60% for Science.

(a) Copy the scatter graph and mark on the final student's results.

(b) Describe the relationship between the Maths result and the Science result.

(c) A student scored 82% for Maths but was absent for the Science exam.
    Estimate a Science result for this student.

* 9 27 students from a Music College go for a drink.
     Their main instruments are either piano,
     violin or cello.

9 of the 15 women play the violin.

$\frac{2}{3}$ of the six piano players are men.

6 men play the cello.

How many students in total play the violin?

* **10** The ages of footballers in two team squads are shown below.

Forest United	
Age	Frequency
19	2
20	4
21	2
22	7
23	1
24	4

Castle Rangers

```
1  | 7 8
2  | 2 2 2 3 3 4 4 5 6 6 7 7 7 8 8 8 9 9 9 9
3  | 0 1 1
```

Key 2|4 means 24

By calculating the mean and range for each team, compare the ages of
the footballers in Forest United with those in Castle Rangers.

* 1   Sam has five cards each with a number on it as shown below.

| 4 | 5 | 7 | ? | ? |

Find the two missing numbers if the mode is 5 and the mean is 6.

* 2

225 g pack of butter	£1.68
Tin of baked beans	57p
2.5 kg bag of potatoes	£1.74
Pint of milk	52p
6 pots of yoghurt	£1.65

Jenny has £3.50 in her pocket. Her mother gives her a £10 note.
She goes to the supermarket and buys items at the prices shown above.

Does she have enough money to buy two 225 g packs of butter,
3 pints of milk, 12 pots of yoghurt, 5 kg of potatoes and 3 tins
of baked beans?

If she has enough money, how much will she have left over after
paying for all the shopping?

If she did not have enough money, how much money did she need?

* 3

Wheato
300 g
£1.44

Wheato
480 g
£2.16

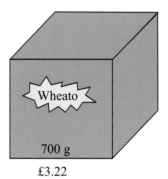

Wheato
700 g
£3.22

The prices of three different sized boxes of cereal are shown above.

Which box offers the best value for money?
You must show all your working out.

* **4** Austin, Layla and Jason are on holiday in Spain. Austin has some money. He gives 20% of the money to Layla.

He gives $\frac{1}{2}$ of the money to Jason.

He now has 450 euros left over.

How many euros did Austin have before he gave some of the money away?

* **5**

A snail and a grasshopper race each other 15 times.

The median time for the grasshopper is 17 seconds and the range for its times is 8 seconds.

The snail's times are shown in the stem and leaf diagram below.

```
7 | 2 6 8
8 | 4 7 8 8
9 | 1 3 5 5 7 8 8 9
```

Key 8|7 means 87 seconds.

Compare fully the times taken by the snail with the times taken by the grasshopper.

* 6 Andy and Kate each travel 80 miles from Andy's house to a shopping centre.
On the way Andy stops for 45 minutes at a Service Station. Kate does not stop
until she reaches the shopping centre. The graph below shows each person's journey.

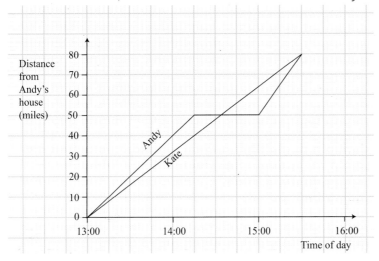

(a) At roughly what time does Kate pass the Service Station?

(b) At what speed does Andy travel from the Service Station to the shopping centre?

* 7 Faith is in Japan and buys her mother a gift costing 11349 yen.

Her brother, Mark, is in the USA and
buys his mother two gifts, one costing $39 and
the other costing $49.92
In pounds, who spent more
money on gifts for their mother
and by how much?

Exchange rates
£1 = $1.56
£1 = 194 yen

* 8

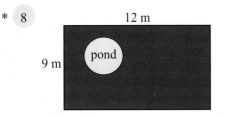

12 m

9 m

pond

The diagram opposite shows the garden of
a new house which has just been built.

The pond has radius 2 m.

The builder needs to put topsoil on the rest of
the garden. The topsoil will be 0.4 m deep.

What volume of topsoil will the builder
need to use? Give the answer to the nearest m³.

* 9

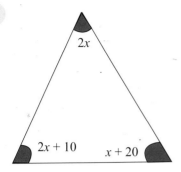

Find the value of x then write down
the actual size of each angle in this triangle.

* 10   Mrs Williams buys her electricity from the Electrogen Company. Her neighbour,
Mr Harris, buys his electricity from the Cotswold Electric Company. They each
receive a quarterly electricity bill as shown below.

Bill for Mrs Williams	Bill for Mr Harris
Previous reading: 12715 Present reading: 13692 Total: £156.32 VAT(5%): £7.82 Total to pay: £164.14	Previous reading: 23187 Present reading: 24312 Total: £168.75 VAT(5%): £8.44 Total to pay: £177.19

Before VAT is added, work out the cost of electricity per unit for each bill.
Which electricity company is cheaper to buy electricity from?

Ⓜ **MIXED 15**

* ① There are 8000 security cameras in a particular city.

35% of the cameras do not work.

The working cameras are found in business buildings, homes and other places in the ratio 5:1:4.
How many working cameras are found in business buildings?

* ② Tanya is helping out on a farm picking cabbages.
Her wage, W, for the day is given by the formula

$$W = 12n + 15$$

where n is the number of boxes of cabbages which she fills.

How many boxes did she fill if her wage for the day was £63?

* ③

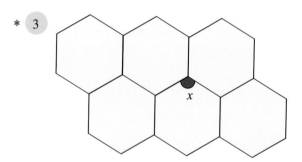

Regular hexagons tessellate (fit together with no gaps).

Calculate the value of angle x.

* 4 (a) Copy the axes below.

Draw the graph of $y = 3x - 2$ for values of x from $x = -3$ to 3.

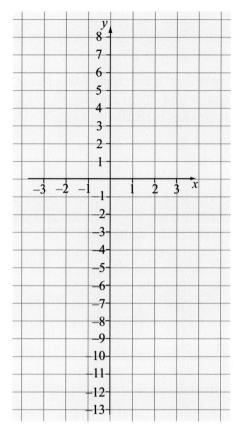

(b) Use your graph to find the value of x when $y = 2.5$

* 5 156 students in Hatton High School are asked which Science subject they liked best.

One third of the 90 boys chose Chemistry.

40% of the 60 students who chose Physics were girls.

27 girls chose Biology.

Find the total number of students who chose Biology.

114

* 6   One day Max sells 20 bacon sandwiches in his cafe for £3.50 each.

For each sandwich he uses 2 slices of bread, 2 rashers of bacon and a small amount of margarine.

The cost of the bread and bacon is shown opposite. In total the margarine and electricity used to make the 20 bacon sandwiches is £3.50

How much profit did Max make on the bacon sandwiches?

Cost price
Loaf of bread £1.20 (20 slices)
Pack of bacon £1.99 (8 rashers)

* 7   Julie lives in Peckford. She wants to spend two hours ice skating in Tenby and at least one-and-a-half hours having a meal and drink afterwards. A bus timetable from Hatton to Tenby is shown below.

Hatton	0950	1030	1130	1230	1330	1430	1450	1530	1550
Marby	1013	1053	1153	1253	1353	1453	1513	1553	1613
Peckford	1025	1105	1205	1305	1405	1505	1525	1605	1625
Neane	1047	1127	1227	1327	1427	1527	1547	1627	1647
Tenby	1105	1145	1245	1345	1445	1545	1605	1645	1705

A bus timetable from Tenby to Hatton is shown below.

Tenby	1535	1635	1735	1835	1935	2035	2135	2235	2305
Neane	1554	1654	1754	1854	1954	2054	2154	2254	2324
Peckford	1616	1716	1816	1916	2016	2116	2216	2316	2346
Marby	1628	1728	1828	1928	2028	2128	2228	2328	2358
Hatton	1650	1750	1850	1950	2050	2150	2250	2350	0020

Tenby ice skating sessions		
	Open	
1100	to	1330
1430	to	1700
1800	to	2030

Julie takes 10 minutes to walk from her home to the Peckford bus stop.

She take 25 minutes to walk from Tenby Bus Station to the ice skating centre.

The table opposite shows when ice skating is possible.

If Julie leaves her home at 1245, what is the earliest bus she might want to catch *home from Tenby*?

If she catches this bus, what time should she arrive home?

Show all your working out fully.

* 8 A small box of chocolates measures
10 cm by 10 cm by 10 cm as shown.

Some of these small boxes of chocolates are
packed into a large box which measures
30 cm × 20 cm × 21 cm.

As many small boxes as possible are packed into
the large box. What is the total value of these
small boxes if one small box of chocolates
costs £5.99?

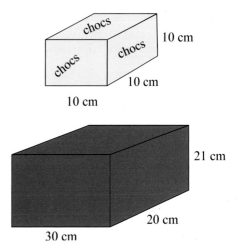

* 9 Colin and five friends want to go to
Athens for a short holiday. Colin finds
the deal below on the internet.

Athens £470 per person for 4 nights
10% off for groups of six people or more
15% off for groups of eight people or more

Special September offer:
20% discount on the price of the holiday
if you travel in September.

What will be the total cost of the holiday
for Colin and the five friends if they travel
in September?

* 10 Candice is researching how often people take the bus. She asks 40 people
in a city and 40 people in a village how often they took a bus in the last week.
The table below shows the results for the city.

City	
Number of bus trips	Frequency
0	12
1	3
2	2
3	1
4	3
5	0
6	1
7	0
8	3
9	0
10	15

The village mean and range is shown below.

Village
Mean = 1.3 bus trips
Range = 10 bus trips

Compare fully the number of bus trips taken by people in the city with
the number of bus trips taken by people in the village.

M | MIXED 16

* 1   Mr. Kennion, his wife and their three children like to swim often each week. They want to buy monthly swimming passes for their local pool.
The prices are shown below:

Monthly pass prices	
Adult	£30
Child	£20
Senior Citizen	£22
Student	£22
Family	£72
(2 adults and 2 children)	

Mr. Kennion works at the pool and so he gets a 30% discount on all prices.

Work out the total he must pay for swimming passes for his entire family.

* 2   The chart shows the shortest distances, in miles, between pairs of cities. For example, the shortest distance between Leeds and Manchester is 44 miles.

Leeds				
190	London			
44	188	Manchester		
212	112	194	Bristol	
139	97	112	82	Birmingham

Sarah sells for a company. She can claim travel expenses of 22p per mile and she can claim expenses for meals. She lives in Manchester. On one journey she travels by car to Bristol then London and then back to Manchester.
She claims for meals costing a total of £33.25 and for the travel expenses.

If Sarah spent a total of £97.47 of her own money on the petrol and meals, what profit does she make from the expenses?

* 3

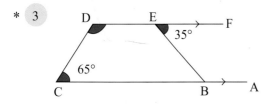

Lines DF and CA are parallel. Work out the value of angle CDE. You must give full reasons for your answer.

* 4   Callum wants to put some wooden coving in his living room.

The wooden coving is 'shaped' wood which is placed where the wall meets the ceiling. Callum wants the coving to go completely around the living room.

The coving is sold in 4 metre lengths. The price is shown below as is a plan of Callum's living room.

coving 4 m lengths
£12.49 each

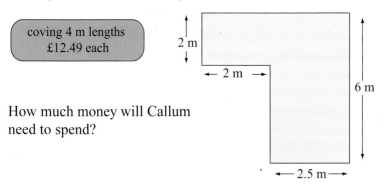

How much money will Callum need to spend?

* 5

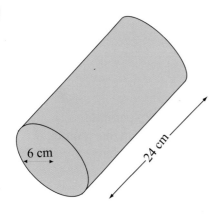

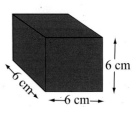

Ruby melts down a metal cylinder of radius 6 cm as shown. She makes as many cubes as possible from the metal. Each cube measures 6 cm by 6 cm by 6 cm.

How many cubes does Ruby make?

Show all your working out fully.

* 6· Several people are asked to count the number of birds they see in their garden each day.

They also record the areas of their gardens.

The information is shown on the scatter graph below.

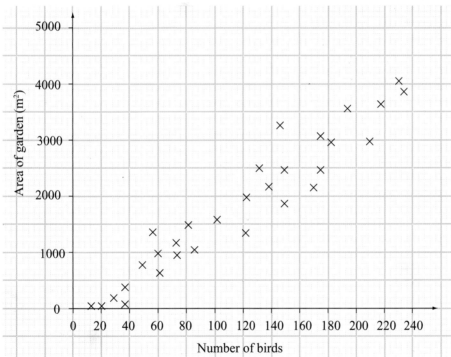

Number of birds

(a) Describe the relationship between the number of birds and the area of the garden.

(b) One person counted 160 birds. Estimate the area of that person's garden.

* 7

4x + 3

2x + 1

The perimeter of this rectangle is 80 cm.
Work out the actual area of this rectangle in cm².

* 8   45 married people are asked where they got married.
The information is shown in the table below.

Place	Frequency
Registry office	16
In another country	4
Church	20
Other places	5

Represent this information in a suitable diagram
or chart.

* 9   Robert, Arjun and Zoe each invest £3000 in shares.
The value of their money rises or falls each year as shown below.

Robert	
Year 1	rises 5%
Year 2	drops 2%

Arjun	
Year 1	drops 3%
Year 2	rises 6%

Zoe	
Year 1	rises 2%
Year 2	rises 1%

The percentage change each year is a percentage of
the amount of money at the start of the year.
Which person has the most money after two years?
Show your working out fully.

How much money do Robert, Arjun and Zoe have in
total after two years?

* 10   Find the value of the length x if the triangle and
the rectangle both have the same area.

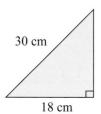

30 cm

18 cm

8 cm

x